BREAKING CONFORMITY

Failure, Performance, Goals, and Dreams

Arthur Greeno and Bryan Smith

DEDICATION

I dedicate this book to all the young entrepreneurs. Those that are like sponges soaking in everything you can to make your dreams successful. I hope this book provides tools for you to know what is truth, and what is myth.

Thank you to my wife Noell for tolerating our late night phone calls while writing this book, and trying to balance my passions and business.

Arthur

This book is dedicated to my beautiful wife Anna and to my kids Legend, Maverick, and Sophia. To you Anna for your love and support no matter what, and for teaching me how to get better in every way. And to our kids. This is for you as well. All of you are the reason I get up and go play every day.

Bryan

TABLE OF CONTENTS

FOREWORD

The best way to communicate and to educate as well as help people see the truth is storytelling. Walt Disney, one of the best storytellers ever, knew this simple concept from the very beginning when he first dreamed up his first animated character, *Oswald the Lucky Rabbit,* which he lost the rights to because of some unexpected legal problems he had not anticipated. Even after losing the rights to Oswald, Walt went on to create *Mickey Mouse* because he knew the secret of success is to never, never, never give up. The rest is history.

Breaking Conformity is a fantastic story that will educate you to understand why you should not believe or accept many common myths at face value, and will also teach you how to make simple myths come true if you also do the hard work that follows many simple statements that make up some of the most popular myths in business today.

Breaking Conformity will teach you the recipe for success through very effective storytelling. To be successful and to achieve your goals, you need to know the whole story about how successful people get more done than other people and how they focus on the details and never quit learning. In fact, the most successful people never quit anything that they really want. They know that everything is hard before it is easy. They know that if they quit, they have lost for sure. You never lose until you give up and quit, no matter how long it takes.

Another important point in this book is to give you a clear understanding on the power of seeking assistance and help with your goals and dreams. You personally don't have to know how to accomplish everything. You can't be an expert in everything. The world is just too complex. Successful people know the value of helping others and also seeking help.

The difference between a dream and a nightmare is in your head. If you think you can, you will. If you think you can't, you won't. Leaders are readers. Don't read this book—study it and reflect on how you need to stop believing every myth and start believing in yourself, and that is no myth.

Lee Cockerell

Former

Executive Vice President,

Walt Disney World® Resort

Lee Cockerell is the Former Executive Vice President of Walt Disney World® Resort and Best-Selling Author of three books: *Creating Magic: 10 Common Sense Leadership Strategies From a Life at Disney, The Customer Rules: The 39 Essential Rules for Delivering Sensational Service, and Time Management Magic: How To Get More Done Every Day.* Today, Lee Cockerell conducts keynote speeches and leadership, management, and customer service seminars around the world. Lee's other resources include his popular weekly podcast, *Creating Disney Magic,* his leadership blog, and his *Creating Magic — Leadership & Coaching on the* Go App. Lee works with the popular online learning site Thrive15. com to deliver creative 15-minute videos on all aspects of business. Lee's books are currently being used as textbooks at colleges and universities across America. Before joining Disney in 1990, Lee held executive positions with Hilton Hotels for eight years and Marriott International for seventeen years before retiring from Disney after sixteen years. For more information, visit www.LeeCockerell.com.

INTRODUCTION

Does it make you nervous to think that many of the things you have learned in your life are wrong?

Leaders use emotional clichéd jargon to make us jump, obey, and temporarily perform better—but will it ever bring long-term success?

This mental poison seeps into other aspects of our lives. It destroys our brain cells. Ask the next person who feeds you one of these clichés if they actually believe it—they most likely do not!

These phrases are myths that only serve to make us feel better for a little while. In truth, these buzzwords don't equal success—they aren't much more than catchy jingles meant to brainwash you into believing that you are happy in your position.

Are you uncomfortable yet?

If comfort is your goal, then success is not in your future.

Can you overcome this? Absolutely, and you can start by shining a light on the lies you have been sold for years—lies that have been sold to all of us!

It's time to commit to seeking the truth, no matter how uncomfortable it may be, for that is the only way to see clearly in this gray world.

What if you could start at the beginning, make a mindset change, and actually train for success?

You can, and by changing your words, you will change your world.

PART ONE

MYTHS DEFINED

Failure
Is Not
an
Option

Bob

"Failure is not an option...
It's a privilege reserved exclusively
for those who try."
-Albert Einstein

It was a cloudy morning, and that was Jack Bryant's favorite way to begin the day. Not that he disliked the sun—he just found that everything easier to see in a black-and-white world.

For the past thirty years, he had chosen to be chauffeured to work in a sleek, black town car. He had tried the subway, he'd tried driving himself, and he'd even tried a taxi, but eventually settled on a chauffeur. Point A directly to point B, no interruptions, and only one pause along the way of his own volition, to get a cup of coffee and a fresh scone.

Driving and parking in the big city have less pleasure associated with the process than the effort warrants. At least, that was Jack's perspective.

Furthermore, Jack was a busy man. The 35-minute commute was highly efficient, like an afternoon uninterrupted by a single phone call. It was a great start to his days.

As a premiere business consultant, he shared office space with the prestigious law firm of Joshua, Dillon, and Morgan. Rumor had it that the first female name would soon be added to the masthead: Isabel, a stellar Hispanic lawyer with an incredible track record—but Jack doubted the firm would ever seriously consider changing the name to Joshua, Dillon, Morgan, and Isabel.

That was just it—people *didn't* change.

And it was because they didn't *want* to change.

That was precisely what kept Jack so busy. As one of the best known and most effective business consultants in the city, his reputation was primarily based on one thing: bringing about change.

Sometimes he felt like he was forcing people, though of course it wasn't a physical battle. Usually it was an acidic verbal barrage that left the patient nearly naked, stripped away of the last vestiges of dignity.

Funny thing, people would often choose to change once there was "no other option."

But it was only when they *chose* it that they really did change.

It was a battle of the wills, and Jack pressed through because he knew the good that was in store for his clients on the other side. In many ways, he felt like he, too, was a lawyer, fighting for truth and justice.

Usually, the individual client and their business would flourish after heeding Jack's advice. The success would make their hesitancy to change a thing of the past. Still, some would refuse to change, and these people would usually crash and burn in an epic failure. Those were the lost cases, and directly the result of not following Jack's advice.

Jack's business advice was spot-on. Maybe he had a bit too much ego, but it came with the territory. At least, that was what he told himself to keep his conscience satisfied.

Situated in an office on the 17th floor, Jack had a steady stream of clients. This translated into a steady stream of prospective clients for the law firm, which is how they partnered together in the first place.

It was a match made in business heaven. They learned to work well together in a truly symbiotic relationship, providing mutual assistance even as they fed off each other.

Mostly, Jack's clients ended up hiring the law firm. Occasionally, it worked the other way around. But since the law firm let Jack rent the office for just one dollar a year, he was not about to complain.

Today, Jack was meeting with Bob Flanery, a businessman with an advertising firm. It just so happened that Bob was the owner's son-in-law, which meant that he *had* to succeed in his new position.

What's more, Bob was to be instrumental in the firm's growth and future.

"That will teach him to marry into the family," Jack muttered to himself. He was reviewing the case notes when the receptionist paged through.

"There is a Bob Flanery to see you," she said with a crisp, professional attitude. His receptionist, Eileen, was a kind-hearted soul in a cold-hearted world.

"Thank you," Jack said in return, punching the button on the black phone on his desk. "Send him on back."

Bob Flanery: 8:04 a.m.

His files showed that Bob Flanery had married the owner's daughter while still in college. He had an MBA and had worked with another advertising agency before landing his current position as VP of operations.

Jack didn't envy young Bob's position.

There was a knock at the door.

"Come on in," Jack said. He didn't get up, just shook hands from where he sat behind his desk.

"Take a seat," he said, pointing to the two leather chairs facing his desk. They were cushioned chairs, like in a psychologist's practice. Since the sessions often took hours, hard wood proved to be a bit too uncomfortable.

Truthfully, Jack had once derived some enjoyment from watching clients squirm on hard chairs. But after a while, Jack could tell that they were paying more attention to their discomfort than his advice, so he begrudgingly upgraded to his current cushioned leather models.

"Now if they squirm, it's because of what I'm saying and not because they are physically in pain," he explained to the office assistant when they made the swap those many years ago. *But I still miss the looks on their faces*, he thought to himself.

Bob was talking.

"Dale, the owner at the firm where I work, is my father-in-law," he explained. "No doubt you knew that, but he insisted that I see you. I can honestly say I don't know why I'm here."

"Yes, Dale and I have been good friends for over twenty-five years now," Jack responded. "Apparently he wanted you and me to get acquainted, and to see if I could help. You see, the position you are stepping into is a very big one. It's do or die, and he wants you to succeed."

"I know," Bob said heartily.

Jack picked up on Bob's mixed pressure and relief that they were already down to business.

"He wants you to succeed…" Jack paused for effect, then added, "…and you *have* to succeed. It's a must. There is no other option for you."

"I *know*," Bob repeated, this time really letting the pressure show.

"So, let's start at the top, shall we?"

"Okay," Bob said. "I was asked to come in as VP of operations and…"

"But you don't deserve it, do you?" Jack interrupted.

"What do you mean?" Bob replied. He was a little upset by the apparent insult, but he had just gotten started. He had prepared his little speech, and he wanted to give it.

"Have you ever held such a big position?" Jack questioned. "Let's put it this way: if you were Dale, would you have hired you?"

"Well, I, uh…" Bob's face glowed a light red, as if he had spent his day amassing a slight sunburn.

"Enough said," Jack stated matter-of-factly, cutting off any further reply from Bob. "That is the starting point. You have a huge task ahead of you for which you may not be well-suited. How's that for pressure?"

Jack found that questions at the end of his stronger statements tended to dial down the pressure or pain inherent to them, while still letting him say what needed to be said.

"Well, I guess I would agree with you," Bob stammered. "It's just that I think I can do the job. I *want* to do the job. But failure is not an option."

Jack paused, his pen about an inch above his paper.

Bob glanced at the clock, then continued, "I still don't know why I'm here. I mean, I've got a job to do and people to direct. I know there is pressure on me to perform. What do you think Dale meant to accomplish by sending me over here?"

"I think I know," Jack said, lowering his pen to the desk. "It could be the fact that I played a big part in Dale's success, in making his business what it is today—but you'll have to get that story from Dale. As far as you and I are concerned, I know exactly why you are here."

"You did? You do?" Bob stammered. He had no idea that Dale owed anything to Jack! And on top of it, he hated not knowing why he was here speaking with Jack.

"Don't worry, I'll tell you why you are here… later," Jack replied. "Until then, I'm going to keep you in suspense!"

"Okay, I guess you have your reasons," Bob acknowledged, obviously a bit unhappy with the way things were going.

"Tell Dale he owes me a dinner, will you?" Jack directed, signaling that the meeting was over.

As Bob stood to leave, Jack added, "There is one thing I want you to do." He handed Bob a long white envelope with the words "200 THINGS I HATE" written across it in capital letters.

"What do I do with this?" Bob asked.

"I want you to do what it says: list at least 200 things you hate," Jack explained. "It's a pretty wide target."

"Okay—I'll work on it," Bob replied, tucking the envelope into his notebook.

Thoroughly confused, Bob stepped out and closed the door behind him. He was not looking forward to his next meeting with Jack the following week. In the meantime, he decided he was going to press Dale for a bit more of the company's history.

Alejandro

T he skies were clear this morning; it would be a sunny day.

His black car pulled to the curb at exactly 7:15 a.m. This had been Jack's schedule for so many years that the private chauffeur company called it the "Jack-Raulbit Route."

"Where is Raul?" Jack asked as the car pulled away from the curb. "How are those stomach ulcers treating him?"

Raul had been Jack's driver for so many years that Jack couldn't remember exactly how long it had been, and Raul had been suffering from stomach ulcers that whole time.

"I'm Alejandro, his nephew," said the new driver in perfect English. "I'll be taking Raul's scheduled routes for a couple of months until he's out of the hospital."

"Hospital? Months?"

"Yes, it was those ulcers he tells everyone about," Alejandro explained. "We were eating at his house over the holidays and suddenly he turned white and ran to the bathroom. Minutes later, we were on our way to the hospital."

"Ouch!" Jack said with an expression of pain on his face. "How did you get his car? I know the chauffeur license is a pretty costly and coveted thing these days."

"We need to keep the car rolling, and I've been with him long enough to know how to do it," Alejandro said as he sped through a long yellow light. "He gets home from the hospital tomorrow, but he can't drive for several months."

"And you've always wanted to be a chauffeur?" Jack asked.

"Well, he told me years ago, 'If I can do it, anyone can.' So I figured I would try it," Alejandro explained.

"Oh, I see," Jack said, settling back in his seat. He liked Raul and felt like he owed him something after countless years of faithful service. And he liked Alejandro's spirit. But he would have to set a few things straight if he were to invest in the relationship.

After all, he would have Alejandro in his car for countless days to come.

"If that isn't a captive audience, I don't know what is," Jack muttered to himself with a sly smile.

Alejandro looked back in the rearview mirror and Jack nodded.

As the car pulled up to the curb outside his office, Jack turned to Alejandro and said, "Thanks. I look forward to talking more tomorrow, and in the weeks to come."

Name It So You Can Claim It

Tricia 3

E ileen was at her post as Jack closed and locked his office door. It was 5:20 p.m. His car would be waiting downstairs in ten minutes.

As he neared the front desk, Eileen motioned for Jack to wait. He pushed the elevator "down" button as she hung up the phone.

"I know you are leaving for the day," she stated, speaking quickly. "But I have a friend who really needs your advice."

"That's pretty nebulous of you," Jack replied, glancing at the elevator lights. It was still at the bottom floor, letting off everyone who had beat him down. He had a few minutes.

"So I took the liberty of planning your ride home," Eileen said with a smile. "Her name is Mrs. Fletcher. She will drive you home today. I just want you to hear her out. Maybe there is something you can do to help her."

"I'm no doctor, as you very well know," Jack replied. He didn't mind the change of plans. It was the unknown element that displeased him.

The elevator light was just starting its slow crawl back up.

"What am I supposed to do for her?" Jack asked.

Eileen looked him in the eye and said, "She's one of those people who think you can write a goal on a piece of paper, tuck it in your wallet, and it will magically become a reality."

Jack's eyes focused. His mind became alert. This was a prominent fallacy, and one that he had shot down many times before.

Eileen was smiling again.

"What?" Jack asked.

"Thank you."

"You think you're pretty sneaky, don't you?" Jack stated.

"It worked, didn't it?"

"Yes, yes it did," Jack said as the elevator door opened. "I'll take the case."

As he descended, Jack wondered what type of resistances Mrs. Fletcher would launch. He already knew what he would say. He would have to lay siege—that was the best place to start in a situation like this.

Mrs. Fletcher was waiting beside a taxi. Apparently, she didn't want to drive and talk at the same time. Jack couldn't blame her.

"Mrs. Fletcher?" Jack asked. "Eileen said you would be down here. I'm Jack. Thank you for the lift home."

"Call me Tricia," Mrs. Fletcher replied as they shook hands and slid into the back seat. The driver already had the address, so he simply hit the road.

"Eileen sings your praises whenever we meet for lunch," Tricia began. "She has so many stories. I don't know how much truth there is to them!"

"That's Eileen for you, always reaching out to help people," Jack replied. The conversation needed to get started. Even with traffic, they would only have forty-five minutes, tops.

After some small talk on various topics, Jack finally felt they were narrowing in on details that would prove useful.

"Life is going great," Tricia was saying. "Several of my girl-friends and I were at my parent's beach house and they were talking about the future, setting goals and things like that."

"How did that affect you?" Jack asked. "I can't imagine you being bothered by discussions about the future."

"Well, I'm not usually bothered at all. I have some friends, like Eileen, who set their sights on something and never let it go until they have achieved it," she replied.

Jack let Tricia talk. Something seemed amiss, and if she didn't come out with it soon, he would have to arrange another meeting. He hated missing details and leaving people unfinished, so one of his few faults (few, he felt) was that he never left a situation unresolved. He fixed it, and if he couldn't, he made sure it was not he who left it undone.

"While we were talking about goal setting, I told my friends about a book I had read many years ago. The author said you should write your goals down and then put them on the mirror in your bathroom or fold them up and put them in your wallet or purse. That has been my approach for years."

"And how's that working out for you?" Jack asked. He tried not to sound too sarcastic, but it was an old incomplete truth—a myth, as he saw it—one that he really didn't like much at all.

"Eileen warned me about you," Tricia said off-handedly, then continued. "It hasn't been that bad. I mean, most of my goals have come true."

"So, what's the problem?" Jack asked. "Did you set a goal that was too big or something?"

"Not really. I have many goals, and have accomplished many of them, but what bothers me are my inner feelings," Tricia admitted.

"Now it's my turn to be confused," Jack replied.

"What I'm saying is that it doesn't feel *right*," Tricia tried to explain. "Something seems missing. Writing the goal on my mirror has worked, or helped, but I think there is more to it."

"You are both right and wise," Jack replied.

"How so?" Tricia asked.

"The fact that you are successful and open to learning, hungry for the truth, sets you apart from the rest," Jack explained.

"There is something more," Tricia confided. "I need to be able to explain myself and my goal-setting process to others, and I can't. That's really why I feel like something is missing—because I can't teach it."

The car stopped at his address.

"Let's continue this another time," Jack said, giving Tricia his business card. "Call Eileen and we can set up a lunch appointment this week."

With that, he slid out and closed the door, and the taxi blended into the sea of yellow.

"That was better than expected," Jack whispered to himself. "I guess I won't be mad at Eileen, and she certainly shouldn't be mad at me!"

I Tried
My Best

Carol

4

The phone rang as Jack was looking out the window at a one-legged pigeon balancing on the ledge outside.

The phone rang again. Most calls went through Eileen at the front desk. Someone must have his direct number, which meant they were probably a friend.

Or a referral.

Jack picked it up. "Hello, this is Jack," he said.

"Hi, Jack, this is Carol," said a voice at the other end. "We haven't met, but I have read about your work for years. I bumped into a friend of yours at an event and he said I should call you. He gave me your number."

"Glad to help a friend of a friend. How can I be of service?" Jack asked, always trying to push to the crux of the matter.

"What I do is manage the hiring at several temp agencies," Carol replied. "You know, where people go to get a job and where companies go to get temporary helpers. Much of the work turns into long-term employment, and of course both the individuals and the businesses want that. That is what I do, but I'm facing two problems that are out of my league."

Jack didn't have anything to say, so he let Carol continue.

"The first problem is that the owner of this temp agency died tragically just a few months ago, and I, as the only person familiar with the systems within the company, was tapped to take over," Carol explained. "But I'll be honest with you—I am in over my head. I have people who report to me, and I need help."

"That is admittedly a tough position to be in, but I'm sure they chose you for a reason," Jack soothed. "You will need a new perspective in your role. Stay calm, work with your team, and I'm sure you'll do fine, especially in this toughest time of transition. As for the second problem, tell me more."

"Well, my second problem is now my biggest focus. It seemed irrelevant at first, but I feel like it is reaching epidemic proportions," Carol went on. "Now that I'm in the field, literally, I'm seeing and dealing with things that I didn't have to before."

"Both problems are very real and we'll have to address them both," Jack responded. "I will need you to give me a bit more information. Tell me more about the second problem?"

"I figured it was just a lack of experience, more of an age-related thing, but now I'm getting it from the teenagers, the 20-year-olds, and even a few 30- and 40-year-olds!" she replied, her exasperation showing through.

"I still don't get it," Jack said, trying not to lose his patience. "What is the exact problem? Is there a sickness spreading?"

"Yes, it's spreading. I call it the I-tried-my-best sickness. It's everywhere, and I can't seem to stop it!" Carol exploded on the phone. "These people are hurting me, and hurting themselves. The businesses are even telling me that they don't want my crews if this is the attitude that comes with them. "

"That sure does sound serious," Jack said, sitting back in his chair. Things were getting interesting. He was beginning to see what Carol was describing. "Sounds like some of them need to be promoted to customer status."

"You mean fire them?" Carol laughed.

"Yes, but if they are all suffering from the same ailment, you have to find out if it's because people don't *care* or if it's because they don't *know*," Jack noted. "If they don't know, then you can train them rather than fire them. I'm guessing that you are dealing with a lot of people who don't know. It's your job, then, to train."

"I was going to say that I don't know how to stop it, but it sounds like some type of training is my answer," Carol continued, almost talking to herself. "I don't live in the city, so we can't meet for lunch, but can I schedule a few sessions with you over the phone?"

"Sure," Jack answered, looking at his open calendar. "I'm free at 2 p.m. on Friday this week, and the same next week. Will that work for you?"

"Yes, it will," Carol replied. "I'll call you—and thank you in advance!"

"I'll pen you in right now," Jack responded as he hung up the phone. He wrote in the time on his desk calendar.

"Believing a lie because you don't know any better—that is frustrating, but forgivable," he said to himself. "Those who believe lies and don't care are another thing completely."

PART TWO

MYTHS BROKEN

Failure Is Not an Option

5

Bob

A t 8:03 a.m., exactly a week after his first brief meeting with Jack, Bob Flanery was waiting in the foyer. Jack would see him shortly.

The previous week had gone by quickly, and Bob was starting to feel like he knew his way around his new position, from the coffee cooler discussions to the parking spaces.

Still, he could not figure out why Dale, his father-in-law and boss, would want Jack to "advise" Bob on anything.

I don't need Jack, Bob thought to himself. *He's good at what he does, I'm sure, but he doesn't know advertising like I do, so what could he offer?*

Eileen put down the phone headset and looked at Bob. "Jack is ready for you now," she said.

Bob put down the book he was absent-mindedly flipping through. Funny, Jack's picture was on the dust jacket.

"Bob, have a good week?" Jack asked, pointing to the cushioned chairs.

"Yes, much the same," Bob replied. He tried to feel competent, but it was a bit tough in this setting, with the leader looking down on him from across the desk.

"Then let's get right into it," Jack said. He clicked his pen as he flipped the case file in front of him closed. "I've got a story to tell you."

"Okay," Bob replied. "I like stories."

"I think you'll like this one," Jack responded. "You no doubt know the Kodak film company. It has been around for longer than you've been alive, but they recently filed for bankruptcy."

"They got left behind as everything went digital," Bob added.

"Oh, you don't know the half of it," Jack exclaimed. "Kodak was a heavyweight in the analog film business, but few know that Kodak missed the boat on digital technology on at least three separate occasions."

"Really?" Bob asked. "I would have thought that, as a company, they would have pushed the envelope to be ahead of the curve."

Jack continued, "Believe it or not, Kodak actually invented digital photography back in 1975. One of their engineers created the first digital camera, but the company put it in a closet."

"What?" Bob stated incredulously.

"In 1995, Kodak brought its first digital camera to market, the DC40. This was years before anyone else got into the digital game, but Kodak never took advantage of its early start. Why? You can imagine, they were steeped in the film business and to embrace digital would mean cannibalizing their existing film business in some ways."

"Thus the hesitancy to jump fully into digital technology," Bob noted.

"Perhaps—but is that an excuse?" Jack countered. "Could a company not do both, and do both well as the landscape changed? But other companies moved faster to fill the niche. Kodak didn't fully rev up its digital business engines until years later when it launched a line of point-and-shoot cameras."

"Film never came back!" Bob muttered out loud.

"And *that* was the key issue," Jack stated forcefully. "But all the while, rivals like Nikon, Sony, Canon, and others kept innovating and growing. Kodak, while it put out good products, was left behind. They could have stayed in their leading position, and if they had, they might be sitting at the top of the pile today."

"Wow, the fact that Kodak invented the digital camera and then put it in the closet for twenty years makes this reality even sadder," Bob stated.

"True, but Kodak's failure to lead and stay ahead of the curve is so very common," Jack replied. "Remember the Atari game company? Or the more recent Blockbuster movie rental business? The list of companies that lost their dominance or disappeared completely is a very long one. Was failure an option for them?"

Bob looked up quickly. "Huh?"

"I think Kodak can and will survive," Jack concluded. "But the company will never be the influencer that it once was, because their competitors have passed them by and because the times have changed so much."

"Well, that certainly was a sad story of failure, market blindness, poor planning, and a whole lot more," Bob said, as Jack seemed to have finished his story. "But I don't work for Kodak. They are an old company. I guess I don't really see how this relates to me and my position."

"Failure was not an option for Kodak, was it?" Jack stated more than asked.

"Well, no, not really. I mean, of course not!" Bob replied.

"And yet they failed, would you not agree?" Jack pressed.

"Yes, I would say they did on a pretty grand scale," Bob acknowledged.

The bottom line

"You are no doubt wondering why Dale sent you to me. Perhaps you are worried that he has some secret agenda for you. Am I right?" Jack asked, flipping open the folder on his desk.

"Actually, that has been bothering me," Bob replied. "No offense, but I don't know why I am here. You aren't in my industry and you don't do what I do."

"Here is the bottom line," Jack answered. "Dale is worried that failure *is* an option for you."

Bob sat there, stunned. His mouth opened, but no words came out.

Jack pointed at Bob's open mouth with his pen, "Oh, you said yourself last week, 'Failure is not an option,' but is it really *not* an option? Failure is always an option, and it's usually the most readily available one!"

Bob snapped his mouth shut, then suggested, "I'm not following you." He was confused and felt pressured, and he didn't like either of those feelings.

"How is that list of 200 things you hate coming along?" Jack asked.

Pulling the envelope out of his notebook, Bob leaned forward and slid it across the desk. Jack caught it and opened the envelope, pulling out two sheets of lined paper.

"There are only 152 things here," Jack noted. "Did I miss another sheet?"

"No, that's all," Bob explained. "That was all I could think of. I'm not really a hateful guy."

"Hmm," Jack hummed aloud. "How is this a reflection of your life? You justify putting three-quarters of your effort into a task, then come up with excuses for why you couldn't complete it?"

"It's just a list!" Bob replied, with a note of exasperation thrown in. "I couldn't think of anything else to add."

"Really?" Jack stated. "So you *do* like mosquitos, skunk smell, child molesters, cheaters, road hogs, English teachers with big red pens…the list is endless."

"Oh, I didn't think of those," Bob confided.

"I said the assignment was very broad when I gave it to you, but you put your own parameters on the list, and so you rationalized a way for you to quit before the job was done," Jack pointed out. "Based on what I see here, failure is an option. If you were not going to finish it, why even waste your time trying? Certainly you could have had other things to do than waste your time on just 152 things you hate."

Before Bob could sputter a reply, Jack brought the conversation back to their current reality.

"Dale stands to lose much more than you do if you fail, and that is a fact," Jack stated. "What he wants—what he *needs*—is for you to do what it takes to *really* make failure not an option."

"But I've already said that it's not an option," Bob replied.

"Based on the results, your list says otherwise...and who at Kodak would have said that failure *was* an option?" Jack asked with a raised eyebrow. "No one likes failure, but if you aren't going out looking for what's new, what's trendy, chasing down every lead, and doing what it takes to be in the know, then you *are* setting yourself up to fail."

Bob sat forward in his chair, trying to figure out what to say next.

"Just saying that failure is not an option doesn't make it true," Jack continued. "You know that."

"Okay, I would agree with that," Bob said, nodding his head. "So what do you propose I do...for both my sake and for Dale's sake?"

Jack smiled. "Now we are ready to begin."

"To start?" Bob replied.

"Yes, and next week I will give you some practical steps to really ensure that failure is not an option. In the meantime, I want you to meet a friend of mine."

"Oh?" Bob asked, glancing around the room.

"His name is Wilson, he's out in the foyer now, and he's eighty years old," Jack noted. "Be nice to him—he was with Kodak for more than forty years. He has forgotten more about advertising than you'll ever learn."

"He was with Kodak?" Bob asked, not sure if that was a good thing or a bad thing.

"His stories will blow your socks off," Jack responded. "Listen and learn, my boy, listen and learn. That needs to be your approach with him."

With that, the meeting was over.

Jack led the way back to the entrance, and after a brief greeting and introduction, he left Bob and Wilson to talk.

An hour later, Eileen paged through the phone intercom. "Jack, they just left."

"Thanks for letting me know," Jack acknowledged. "How did it go?"

"You know Wilson, it was pretty animated," Eileen chuckled. "But I think Bob was listening. I heard Wilson tell him three or four times that you can still miss your goal even after preparation and execution, and that true failure only happens when you quit."

"Good news and good teaching; thank you," Jack said, pushing off the intercom button.

"I just hope Bob learned something," he whispered to his computer as he went back to his typing.

If I Can Do It, Anyone Can

Alejandro

6

Jack was downstairs at 7:15 a.m., waiting under the green canvas-covered entrance to his apartment. Alejandro was late.

Looking down the street for his black car was futile, as there were countless numbers of them coming and going in every direction, so he just waited.

A full ten minutes later, Alejandro pulled up and Jack swiftly jumped in the back seat.

"I'm sorry I'm a bit late," Alejandro said over his shoulder. "Traffic, some days it's bad and some days it's worse."

"How's Raul?" Jack asked. He wasn't as bothered by the time factor as he was by Alejandro's insincere apology. If your intention is to be on time, then leave early enough to cover any unexpected delays—that was Jack's modus operandi, and he accordingly had plenty of time to arrive at his office; his first appointment wasn't scheduled until 9 a.m. Still, Raul was never late, and Jack did not appreciate falling behind schedule.

Alejandro glanced in the mirror and answered as he pulled into traffic, "Raul comes home today. I'm picking him up right after I drop you off."

"Tell him I'm hoping he rests and feels better soon," Jack responded.

"I'll do that," Alejandro acknowledged. "Say, what was it you wanted to talk about, anyway? You left me hanging yesterday; I was wondering what was on your mind."

"Funny you should ask," Jack said, leaning forward in his seat. "It's not really what's on my mind, but what is on your mind."

"How so?" Alejandro asked.

"You said that Raul had told you, 'If I can do it, anyone can.' I'm not questioning you, and maybe you do indeed want to be a chauffeur, but what if it's not the job for you? Have you considered that?"

"Well, not too much," Alejandro admitted. "If Raul can do it, I know I can do it as well."

"That might be true," Jack acknowledged, and then paused. "And it might *not* be true."

"I'm a bit confused," Alejandro confessed.

"I thought you might be," Jack stated, fully intending such an effect. "Let me tell you a story while you drive. Are you good with that?"

"Okay," Alejandro accepted.

"Several years ago, I was asked to address 500 sales reps who worked for the largest real estate company in America," Jack began. "They wanted me to motivate them, and though I'm not Mr. Motivator, someone apparently thought I might be able to deliver a message that would help the newer agents perform better with a little increased raw determination. In short, they hoped I would pump them up! I started by talking about having a winning attitude. I told them to work on becoming someone worth imitating."

"I like that," Alejandro broke in. "And I am new to this, so I like what you are saying."

"Good, that's great," Jack affirmed, knowing that Alejandro was not getting it. "I told them that they were in the room that day because of a decision they had made yesterday. I went on to tell them to focus on not letting their weaknesses damage their future income earning potential."

"That's good, too," Alejandro quipped as he passed a moving truck traveling too slowly in the left lane.

"I closed by telling them that the path to their greatest success would most likely take them through their greatest fear," Jack continued. "Then I said, 'No doubt you have all heard the phrase, "If I can do it, anyone can?" Well, I won't leave you with that idea today because I don't believe it and I think it's false.'"

Alejandro didn't say anything, but stole a quick glance in the mirror before riveting his eyes ahead.

Looking squarely in the mirror, Jack stated, "Every successful real estate agent in that room was successful because they went after it and got it done. Do you think each of those 500 people were wired with the same amount of determination, ability, and raw talent?"

After a slight pause, Alejandro shook his head and acknowledged, "No, it would be impossible. With that many people, no doubt many of them were go-getters, but they couldn't all be at that high level."

"Exactly," Jack responded, thankful that Alejandro was at least keeping up with him. "But with passion and determination, one can cover up a lot of missing ability and talent. It is a recipe for disaster to simply assume that you can do what another person is doing. Clearly, it's not as simple as just believing that you can do something as well as another person. You just said that it's statistically impossible, didn't you?"

"Yes, I did, and I guess I would have to agree with that," Alejandro nodded.

"Here is the funny part," Jack chuckled aloud. "I walked off stage and went to the back of the room to grab some water before I left. Who should walk on stage after me? The owner of the company! I was interested in what she had to say, so I loitered around the water cooler for a few more minutes. As she spoke, everyone cheered and clapped in excitement. She wasn't saying anything very exciting, but clearly many people in the audience were trying to impress upon her that they loved every word of it."

"Sucking up to her," Alejandro stated. "That's what they were doing. I've seen that in classrooms and in group settings and in businesses."

"Right you are!" Jack replied with enthusiasm. "But then she said it! She looked at the sea of faces and proclaimed, 'I just want all of you to know that if I can do it, anyone can.' That was a bold-faced lie!"

"How so?" Alejandro asked. "And wasn't it a bit awkward, since you had just poked holes in that exact concept only a few minutes earlier?"

"I don't think she listened to anything I said," Jack stated. "But the audience was falling over themselves to prove that they loved everything she had to say—so they weren't really listening either. Want to know why it was a lie?"

"Yeah, I would like to know," Alejandro repeated. His brows were furrowed like he was deep in thought.

"She had been given the company," Jack explained. "The company was already successful when it was handed to her. She didn't really do anything, and she certainly never sold a single piece of real estate herself. She hadn't done what her sales reps were doing. The truth was, her little 'if I can do it, anyone can' phrase was only about getting those new real estate agents to make an emotional decision about their situation in the hopes that they would try to perform better. It was a pep rally, nothing more."

"Oh, I see," Alejandro said quietly from the front seat.

"Keep your eyes on the road," Jack ribbed from the back seat. "I know your mind is elsewhere, and that is good."

The morning's ride was almost over. Jack checked his watch—it didn't look good.

"The whole 'if I can do it, anyone can' myth is so blatantly false that it actually makes me want to laugh whenever I hear it," Jack added, slapping the back of the front seat. "But seriously, as you and I both know, there is no way we can all do the same things—because we are not all willing to work as hard, to take the same risks, or to be as determined. Some of this is learned behavior, and some is our God-given natural ability."

"Ain't that the truth," Alejandro acknowledged. He was thinking, and driving a bit slower than normal.

Jack sat back in his seat. He always got a bit passionate about things, but he truly cared. He was also now truly late, and that wasn't a good way to start the day.

"Here we are," Alejandro said as he finally pulled to a stop at Jack's office. "Sorry we're late."

"Next week, you and I are going to sit down for a coffee and scone together," Jack added, picking up his black leather briefcase. "I don't want you thinking too hard while you're driving!"

With a wave, he was out of the cab and on his way to the front doors of the office building.

"What's up with that?" Alejandro asked himself when he was alone. He put the meter on "occupied" and headed to the hospital.

"Everything I thought was solid about my plans has just been shaken. I'm not sure I like that man!"

The black car was long gone by the time Jack reached his office. He seldom communicated with Raul outside of their professional relationship, but today he wanted to send him a text, both to welcome him home and to say that Alejandro was a bright young man.

"It helps to talk nicely to their heads while I'm chipping away at their feet," he said aloud.

The day was off to a roaring start. Being ten minutes late wasn't the end of the world.

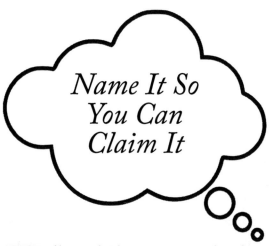

*Name It So
You Can
Claim It*

7

Tricia

E ileen had set up a lunch meeting between Jack and Tricia for today, and it was already 11:45 a.m.

The phone buzzed its interoffice buzz. "Just making sure you remembered your lunch appointment with Tricia today," Eileen said.

"I'm leaving now," Jack replied. Eileen and Tricia had been friends for years, which Jack knew meant that Eileen was watching!

As he walked to the front waiting area to call up the elevator, Jack glanced back at Eileen, who seemed to be hiding behind the lamp on her desk, and said, "I know what you are thinking."

Startled, Eileen responded, "What?"

"You are thinking that you have taken a big risk introducing me to Tricia, and you are worried that I'll make her so mad that she'll refuse to talk to you again," Jack summarized. "How close am I?"

Red-faced, Eileen admitted, "That is all true—so don't mess this up!"

"I'll try not to," he called over his shoulder as he stepped into the elevator. "Pressure, pressure!"

On the way down, Jack held his thin leather folder tightly to his chest to avoid having it bent or knocked out of his hands by the countless other people jammed in the elevator. His leather folder, held together with magnets, was ideal for face-to-face encounters and for walking down the streets in blustery weather.

Outside, Tricia was waiting as planned. "I know this quiet bistro just a few blocks over, if that sounds good to you?"

"Sounds ideal," Jack replied.

As they walked, Jack looked for a way to start their conversation. No point in waiting until they were eating.

Tricia beat him to it.

"What I want to know," she began, "is the whole goal-setting process, from beginning to end. I want to know how it really works."

"It's great, and necessary, to fully understand what you are asking for, but you need to see what's wrong with the old system first," Jack clarified.

"Okay, I'll go with that," Tricia said as they walked, weaving between pedestrians and bicyclists.

"Who needs a doctor the most?" Jack asked. "It's the person who realizes he or she is sick. If you need a regular checkup, you can reschedule for some other time, but if you are sick, you will beat the doors down to be treated!"

Tricia nodded in agreement.

"That's a mindset, an I-will-not-be-denied mindset, which is also important in the goal-setting process. There is no goal that cannot be accomplished when the person refuses to be distracted. It's a 'done deal,' as they say, long before the goal is in hand. It's getting up off the mat once more than your opponent."

Stepping out of the flow of traffic and up to the door of the bistro, Jack asked, "You may be wondering what happened to the goal that was written on the card and then stuck in the wallet?"

"Yes, I guess so," Tricia acknowledged, a perplexed look across her face.

As they were ushered to their reserved table, Jack explained, "The determination of the I-will-not-be-denied person is just one element of goal setting. It's not everything, but it is a very big part. In the same way, writing a goal down and tucking it in your purse is only a part of the process. In fact, it's a much smaller part of the process than most people will ever know, much less admit."

"How so?" Tricia asked, thankful that he didn't nail her to the wall for her obvious lack of knowledge. He was being tactful, and she appreciated that.

"Most people think goal setting is magical, instant, requires no effort, and happens right on schedule," Jack summed up.

"True," Tricia responded with a furrowed brow. "But in the real world, in the trenches, where business takes place, I know it's not the case. But how the goal setting really happens? I don't think I could define it for you."

"In time, you will," Jack encouraged. "Right now, however, you are beginning to see just how far away we are from the truth. Before we make things clear, I want to muddy the waters a bit more for you."

Making it plain

"How so?" Tricia repeated.

"Statistics show that people who write down their goals have more than an 80% higher success rate in achieving them," Jack stated, barreling forward. "Which makes it seem like the mysterious process of writing the goal down and putting it in your purse is incredibly effective…but not so!"

Tricia was taking notes and glanced up with a "please go on" look on her face.

"The 'name it and claim it' approach to goal setting is to do just that: name the goal and claim it, like writing it down and stuffing it in your magical purse," Jack explained, sarcasm dripping off his last words. "Doing this is nothing more than claiming that something they want is already theirs, which doesn't make it so."

"Surely we need to name the goal, do we not?" Tricia asked, struggling to find something to stand on mentally.

"Of course," Jack replied. "But there is much more to it. I see people write a goal on a business card, put it in their pocket, and it's never seen again. What a waste! The act of writing down a goal is merely step number one in the process. It's just the first step of many."

"I can see that," Tricia acknowledged. "You muddied the waters for me, what else?"

"Another factor is your thinking," Jack went on. "The late Zig Ziglar, famous salesman and motivational speaker, called it 'stinking thinking.' It's where we allow a lie or half-truth to rattle around in our subconscious minds for so long that we begin to believe it."

"Ouch, that about nails everyone to the wall," Tricia pointed out.

"Precisely, but when it comes to goal setting, and other important foundational truths, we had better get it right," Jack noted.

"Ain't that the truth!" Tricia quipped.

"Napoleon Hill wrote about how the subconscious mind is related to our dominant thoughts in his book *Think & Grow Rich*," Jack explained. "He described our minds as 'fertile garden spots' that will grow weeds in abundance if we don't purposefully plant something else there."

"So stuffing my goal in my purse and forgetting about it is probably not going to get the weeds out of my garden," Tricia said, trying to follow the logic of the metaphor.

"Yes, you could say that," Jack noted with a smile. "But the absence of something is not enough. You need to purposefully fill it, or plant it in this analogy, so that your subconscious mind can work and grow on your behalf. Regarding your goals, if you fill your mind with the outcome you are looking for, you will subconsciously tend to look for similarities and identify opportunities as they arise."

"That sounds amazing," Tricia stammered, "but I have no idea what you just said."

"I'll use a true story about a client from years ago that will help this make more sense," Jack replied. "This client had dreamed since his teen years of owning a Ford Mustang. Not just any Mustang, but a 1969 Shelby Fastback—the sleek design, the rumble of the muscle, and the smell of gasoline when you revved it."

"Sounds sexy!" Tricia joked.

Their food arrived, and partway through their meal, Jack continued with his story. "Once my client grew older and married, and business was trucking along, his wife actually bought him a 1969 Fastback. It was forty years old, and he felt every second of that span every time he started it. After quite a few maintenance projects on his dream car, he realized that he didn't have time to invest in his beauty like it deserved."

"Death of a dream? Or maybe a goal deferred?" Tricia asked between bites.

"Not entirely, and though there is a time and a place to put a goal on pause or to scratch it from your list altogether, in this case it was something else," Jack noted, then went on. "My client still wanted a unique nostalgic muscle car, but he wanted it all to be new and running like a dream."

"You can't have it both ways," Tricia laughed. "Sounds like a serious midlife crisis to me."

"Perhaps," Jack offered, trying to steer the story back on track. "But he found a picture of his dream car, printed it out, and taped it on both his office wall and his bathroom mirror. At work, everyone who saw it asked why it was there, and that led to quite a few discussions. All of his friends and colleagues knew about his '69 Fastback."

"Sounds a lot like a goal stuffed in a purse, but on his wall and mirror," Tricia ribbed.

"Yes, and I told you I'm trying to muddy your waters, so let me continue," Jack jabbed in return. "One day, a friend called and said, 'I found your car.' It turns out there was a company that would build exactly what my client wanted: an ideal, vintage muscle car that would also run like a dream. So my client flew up there, saw their operations, and ordered his car."

"I can see how the idea for his car, stuck on his mirror and discussed with his friends, was some of that subconscious thinking you mentioned a bit ago," Tricia acknowledged. "But there has to be more. Otherwise it's only a slight variation on naming and claiming it."

"Oh, there is more, much more," Jack said in return. "In addition to putting the car picture up and sharing his desire with a few close friends, my client started doing something amazing!"

"Which was…? Come on, tell me," Tricia pleaded, knowing that Jack was baiting her along.

"He started saving money," Jack stated matter-of-factly. "I know, sounds incredibly practical, but goal setting is more nuts and bolts than pixie dust. My client saved $150 per month and then upped it to about $250 per month. Years later, when the opportunity came for him to buy his dream car, he was ready to take action—and he bought it."

"Wow, now that really *is* practical," Tricia noted with sincerity. Jack could almost see her brain beginning to sort through her preconceived ideas and weeds related to goal setting.

Their meal was done. It had been a success on all fronts, Jack hoped.

"So the 'write the goal and put it in your purse' approach, would that be sufficient to make his Mustang dreams a reality?" Jack asked.

"Obviously not," Tricia stated emphatically. "I'm thoroughly confused and liberated at the same time. All of it, from your client putting that picture on his mirror to sharing the desire with his friends to saving money, it all played a part."

"Or to think of it another way," Jack added, "when you take a piece of paper and write goals down and then fold it up and put it away, you have to realize that no matter what you might have heard some traveling motivational speaker say, those goals will not unfold in the same way that you folded them. A good part of the strategy is planning, determination, passion, unbelievable work ethic and drive, accountability, and market testing."

"How true!" Tricia replied.

"Then would you say that the myth of naming and claiming, of writing a goal on a piece of paper and stuffing it in your purse to wait until it magically comes to pass, is sufficiently broken?" Jack asked.

"Totally," Tricia responded.

"Good, I was hoping so," Jack concluded. "And next week we'll discuss more specific corrective measures. We broached this today, as your notes testify and as you have just explained back to me, but next week I'll give you the whole goal-setting process that you're looking for."

"Sounds great," Tricia exclaimed. "Same place?"

"Yes, I'll meet you here at 11:45 a.m. next week," and with that, Jack excused himself and headed back to his office.

The walk would help to clear his head. Tricia's head was so full that it would probably take her several days to process it all.

"At least I hope so," Jack mumbled to himself. "Drowning her with reality was my plan. Now I just need to know if Eileen has any feedback."

A short ten minutes later, Jack felt the jolt of the elevator and heard the "ding" of the bell as he reached his floor. Stepping out, he noticed Eileen, her neck tipped to the side, talking animatedly into the phone.

Slipping past, he opened his office door and sat his leather folder on the corner of his desk. Right in the middle of his desk lay a full bar of dark Toblerone chocolate! Beside it was a small note from Eileen.

It read:

"This was either going to be a dagger or a piece of chocolate. I'm glad it's chocolate. Thank you—Tricia says she's pleased."

Eileen smiled. She could hear Jack laughing from where she sat.

I Tried
My Best

Carol

8

The phone rang on Friday at 2 p.m. Jack had been expecting the call.

"Jack, thank you for taking the time," Carol began.

"Glad to," Jack replied. "How goes the battle against the 'epidemic' as you described it the other day?"

"It's much the same," Carol answered. "But now my ears pick it up from a hundred yards away. Every time I hear someone stammer 'I tried my best,' I have to be careful not to hyperventilate!"

"Be patient as you bring this ship around," Jack encouraged. "Eventually, you'll be sailing in a whole new direction."

"I sure hope you're right, but at the moment, I feel like I'm drowning, and I don't know where to start cleaning up this mess," Carol stated in a voice dripping with sadness and frustration.

"Let's look at it this way," Jack began. "You are truly aware, like a doctor is aware. You know what's wrong and you see how people are affected. You need to quarantine it, treat it, and then train others to do the same."

"Yes, I guess that's one way to look at it," Carol responded.

"Okay, then you and I are like two doctors," Jack continued with his analogy. "We are going to examine the problem together, discuss the cure, and then you are going to take it to your patients."

"I like that approach," Carol replied. "It's truly out of my league. I've never experienced something like this. If it isn't contained soon, a lot of lives and businesses are going to be negatively affected."

Call it what it is

"We must start by describing it in detail," Jack began. "Call it what it is, with no worries that we'll offend anyone. To that end, I'll start. The 'I did my best' statement is just a myth that should be left unsaid 99% of the time. If you truly tried your best, it would be obvious to us—but saying you did makes us think you failed, and could have tried harder. This phrase was crafted by the same people who created the Participation Award!"

"So well said!" Carol responded with enthusiasm. "I must add that the 'I tried my best' statement is a way of justifying failure. If I hear, 'I didn't get the job, but I tried my best' one more time, I think

I'll strangle someone. It's never the truth, and for some reason, those who say it are oblivious to that very obvious fact!"

"When 'I tried my best' is actually the truth, that small 1% of the time, people really don't want to hear it," Jack pointed out. "When was the last time you saw someone get an award and say, 'I tried my best, and…it worked!' Anyone who said that would be thought of as an egotistical jerk."

"Speaking from years of experience, there are occasionally times when a required task is above someone's ability," Carol noted. "They truly may try their best and fail. What do you do then?"

"When this happens, the answer is reaching above our best," Jack explained. "When it comes to success, change things up a bit so the phrase is a question. Ask yourself, 'Did I try my best? If I tried my best and it didn't work, what are the next steps? Can I make an extra sales call? Can I try it another way? Is there someone better at this who will give me advice?' So many ways to actually get it done."

"That is great practical advice," Carol commented. There was a pause as she typed furiously on her computer, her keys making a steady clacking sound.

About a minute later, Jack spoke up, "Any of our remedies or teachings can be studied and turned into talking points, things that your temp force will get, understand, and apply."

"Oh, that's my exact plan," Carol exclaimed as more clicking and clacking came through the phone receiver.

"Based on your experience in the real world, do you see this to be a generational problem?" Jack asked.

"I would say it is," Carold stated matter-of-factly. "You don't hear many old-schoolers talking this way. It's more of a new-school mindset that primarily plagues the teens and 20-year-olds, but that of course affects everyone in every business that employs this generation."

"Life isn't just about showing up, and whiners don't win," Jack noted, as if to himself. "All of this getting a trophy just for showing up, all these consolation prizes, don't mean anything in the game of real life."

More clicking from Carol's end. Finally, she said, "Why do we encourage our kids to try their best? Are we just tricking them into thinking that they are actually capable?"

"Maybe they are capable, but just lazy?" Jack added, keeping the reasoning going. "Trying your best should never be an excuse to slack off. Making a decision and committing to excellence should be the goal. We can't always control the results, but we can control our effort and activity—so there is no *trying*, only doing. People who are trying to do their best have not yet decided if they will succeed or not."

"Is this a problem we created as a society?" Carol pondered. "With all our entitled thinking. Should everyone get a raise? A promotion? Win the big game? In my world, it doesn't work that way."

"Those who suffer from this 'I did my best' scourge are really failing to fit into the real world," Jack replied. "Is that not the truth?"

"It is certainly the truth," Carol reiterated.

"And since that is the case," Jack continued. "Instead of creating an environment where people need to say 'I tried my best' in their failure, we should tell them, 'Don't worry about it. Sometimes we fail, sometimes we lose. If you choose to play the game, you will strike out sometimes.' There is no reason to say 'I tried my best' amidst failure. Winners are always trying their best, and their best is assumed to be the baseline—but they don't always win, and that's okay."

"I wish people would stop just trying to do and actually do their best," Carol explained. "And if they fail, they get back up and get after it. That would make a world of difference…and that would be someone worth imitating."

"Well, Doctor Carol, I think we are crossing over into remedies for the ailment you are witnessing," Jack said. "Let's talk more about that next week. Remember, failing never happens until you quit."

"I have a lot to study at this end," Carol replied.

"Keep doing research and let's meet next Friday as planned," Jack concluded. "We'll come up with a plan of action that will turn your ship around."

"Sounds good to me," Carol said. "Thank you, and till next time."

The phone call was over.

Jack's 2 p.m. appointment was now over, but he had a long list of notes and details to arrange and organize. The disease running rampant in Carol's city was no doubt alive and well across the nation.

That was a thought worth pondering. Preparation for the future calls he would undoubtedly receive on this topic made good business sense.

PART THREE

---•◦•---

MYTHS
FIXED

Bob

9

Failure Is Not an Option

At 8:00 a.m., Bob found himself in the same cushioned chair in Jack's spacious office on the 17th floor. Another week had gone by, and it had been an enlightening week at that.

"Thank you again for your time," Bob said as he shook Jack's hand.

"How was your week?" Jack asked. The customary question seemed to have more meaning this time.

"I'm seeing things differently," Bob admitted. "In my own thoughts and in the words of others around me. I'm beginning to wonder if failure really is an option."

"Maybe even a bit scary?" Jack added.

"Yes, and if I were Dale, my boss, I think I would be worried as well," Bob responded.

"Empathy, that's a good sign," Jack said as he made a note in the case folder on his desk. "Today, we are going to outline action steps that you can take to make sure that failure is not an option for you."

Bob had his notepad out. He was prepared. A thought zipped through his mind: *The atmosphere seems more open; less antagonistic than usual. Almost as if the wall of defensiveness has come down, and now Jack is simply giving me his wisdom and practical insights!*

Then he wondered, *The wall of defensiveness...I think that was my own wall.*

"Ready?" Jack asked, interrupting Bob's internal processing.

"Yes, let's do it," Bob responded.

Failure Reason #1

"The first reason for failure is thinking that our words form some sort of powerful wall of fairy dust around us," Jack began. "The fact is, failure is always an option! Statistically speaking, I give most businesses a 50/50 chance of surviving a few short years from their genesis. Am I being negative, a naysayer, or unkind? No, I'm not. That's just the way it is. And for those who don't make it, I don't think they were ever walking around saying that failure was an option, do you?"

Bob didn't look up. He was writing, and thinking of his own choice of words.

"Honestly, my heart aches to see so many businesses, companies, and families hurt and torn apart each year due to failure…being an option," Jack explained.

All Bob did was nod as his pen kept going. He hadn't been sure if Jack actually cared about anything or anyone. This was news—maybe Jack did care.

Failure Reason #2

"Here is where things start to get really personal," Jack explained. "The next reason for failure is probably the saddest, because it is so preventable: people lack self-control. Every one of us has some kind of self-control issue. Some people will argue and deny it, but in reality, everyone does."

Bob was about to say something, but then decided not to interrupt.

"I once had a business owner, sitting right where you are now, tell me that while he was getting his business started, he was also into video games. He would purchase a new game, stay up all night playing it, and then go to work the next day."

"I'd call that an 'unproductive day,'" Bob added.

"Oh, without a doubt," Jack agreed. "But sadly, he would repeat this day after day. He would go home, eat dinner, get back on his computer, and do it again. He did it until he conquered the game."

"Why? Who cares if you beat the game or not?" Bob said, shaking his head.

"That's your take on this, but clearly the urge to play video games is not a self-control issue for you," Jack stated. "Thankfully, this businessman came to his senses. He realized it was negatively affecting his work, his family, his wife, and his very future."

"How did he come to his senses?" Bob asked. "Did his wife slap him upside the head?"

"No, but she should have," Jack replied with a smile. "In truth, what broke him free was an exercise that I assigned to him. I told him, 'Track your day in 30-minute increments, then come back to me next week with a full report.' He did, and he was a changed man!"

"That's interesting," Bob replied, imagining how that revelation must have felt.

"Oh, it was!" Jack chucked. "He laid that well-worn tracking sheet on my desk and started to cry, literally. The realization that he had been spending more hours in a week playing video games than on growing his business, much less spent with his wife and kids, hit him like a ton of bricks! He chose right then and there to invest in his business and his family. What good is the phrase 'failure is not an option' if you are self-sabotaging your own future?"

"Wow," was all Bob could say.

"So, Bob," Jack said, leaning forward in his chair, his elbows resting on the desk. "I really need to ask you this: What are some areas where your lack of self-control is affecting your stated reality of failure not being an option?"

Bob's mouth opened, but Jack cut him off.

"I don't want an answer here, this is no shrink session!" Jack declared loudly. "That's for you to ponder and bring back next week. I've heard answers like eating, family boundaries, blaming others, gambling, chocolate, sex, drinking, exercise, anger, beating yourself up, smoking, and on and on the list goes. I have practically heard it all, and the point is that if you are unbalanced, you could absolutely be setting yourself up for failure—and that, sadly, is why failure is always an option!"

"Let me add one more thing," Jack continued. "At times, in order to thrive, you will need to put in more than the normal 40-hour week. Henry Ford instituted a 40-hour week in his factories to increase productivity and because he felt that two days off for rest or leisure should not be reserved for the wealthy. If you are trying to get ahead or outpace others, you may need to put in more time than everyone else. How much time are you willing to put into your success? It takes a lot of inertia to get a flywheel going, but once that happens, you can sit back a little. Usually, however, if you never put that initial energy into getting it started, it will never happen."

Failure Reason #3

"The third reason for failure is that people lack the courage to ask for help," Jack said, as if pondering something. "You have heard the phrase, 'No man is an island entire of itself,' haven't you?"

Bob nodded.

Jack continued, "At the surface, it's a silly phrase, because people aren't islands and never could be. And at the surface level the island may look small, but go below and you see how huge it really is.

Remove the base and you have nothing. The point is, we need each other. There are a lot of people under and beside a successful person."

"I've often wondered why we as humans need hugs and physical touch from others, but it makes sense now," Bob said. "We do in fact need each other, probably more than we think."

"Exactly," Jack responded, glad that Bob was on the same wavelength, because now he wanted to push him a bit further. "According to researchers, a sympathetic touch from a doctor leaves people with the impression that the visit lasted twice as long. It's in us—we want to connect. Now, you may or may not believe me, but I have literally asked hundreds of people for guidance, advice, assistance, connections, money, wisdom, strength, help, friendship, jobs, favors, promotions, time, discounts, forgiveness, trust, and even prayers."

Bob wasn't sure if what he heard was true. Jack seemed so solid, so full of answers, so complete, so…so much like an island to himself!

"I'm not an island to myself," Jack said with a hint of a smile, "and neither are you. I may ask for things from other people, but I rarely consider what they think of me—that is none of my business. Only a handful of times have people refused to give me what I asked for. Why? Because we are wired to help each other. They want to, and it's to your benefit if they do."

Failure Reason #4

"The fourth reason for failure combines a lack of self-control with secluding ourselves. I call it 'going turtle.' Basically, when things are not going right, we go inward and avoid other people."

"But that's so easy to do," Bob blurted out. "It's tough, at least for me, to pick myself up and engage with people after I've just fallen down."

"Yes, and very natural—yet very deadly," Jack noted. "The act of 'going turtle' could look like many different things, such as watching too much TV, spending a lot of time in the bar, getting drunk, or even sleeping. It's hiding, often away from people, with the hope that an obvious lack of self-control item, such as drinking, will in some way tide you over while the situation somehow rights itself. Of course, it doesn't fix anything."

Bob pointed out, "They probably wouldn't argue that their lack of self-control could lead to a fix, but they do it anyway. Their desire to 'turtle,' as you call it, overrides what they know to be true."

Keeping the discussion going, Jack added, "Ideally, this is the place where a spouse or friend can step in and slap you silly!"

"Yes, well said," Bob laughed, but he knew it was true.

Failure Reason #5

"The fifth reason for failure is something that you will no doubt have to battle with as a leader," Jack went on. "It is the act of people-pleasing, and in your case, it could mean spending too much time letting employees or customers run your business."

Bob was about to ask a question, but Jack was on a roll, "No, I don't mean letting a team of high-performing people run a section or project. You want and need that. Let me give you a good example of a bad case. I had a business owner doing things that did not make any business sense at all. When I pushed him for answers, he said that his customers liked it that way. After more research, I found that it was not necessarily how all his customers liked it, but rather the way a few of his more pushy, obnoxious, verbal customers liked it. They had beaten the owner into submission and he complied so he wouldn't have to hear their complaints anymore! That is people-pleasing for you."

Jack paused, then looked across his desk at Bob and asked, "Now, is that a good way to build a profitable business?"

"Of course not!" Bob exclaimed.

"Do you do that?" Jack jabbed. "How do you not do that? Do you let that happen under your watch? And under what circumstances would you justify doing that? Sometimes people need to know that the word 'no' is a complete sentence!"

Bob made more notes. He had much to think about, and no doubt a painful self-examination to bring to Jack next week.

"Getting the hint?" Jack said, as if talking to his files. "Failure is more of an option than we often realize."

Failure Reason #6

"The last reason for failure that I want to mention today is the fact that many people think they know it all. I know you find that hard to believe," Jack said with a chuckle, "but they have come to the conclusion that there is nothing else to learn."

"And that hurts the business!" Bob stated with enthusiasm.

"You speak from experience?" Jack asked.

"Oh, you should have seen my last boss," Bob went on. "He was the most arrogant man I have ever met. He told me once, 'Everything you know about marketing, you've learned from me.' Sadly, he taught me nothing that I actually wanted to remember. He was surrounded by people who were passionate, hungry, and talented, and yet no good ideas ever made it past his desk. He thought only his own ideas were worth anything. Reminds me of the Kodak story you told me last week."

"Yes, exactly," Jack continued. "Given enough time, all systems will fail. It's like metal on a ship at sea: eventually, it's going to rust. I knew a young man who worked on a beautiful ship built in 1953 that had more paint in some places than metal! Eventually, without work and effort, every ship, car, factory, or business will fail. Even a business that is functioning incredibly, given enough time, will start to see parts not functioning so well, and eventually it will fail."

"This is an easier one for me," Bob stated. "I know from experience that this is true. My last boss had pretty much scuttled the business by the time I left. What had been working smoothly a few short years earlier was taking its last gasps for air when I moved here."

"Lucky you left when you did," Jack said as he made a note on the paper on the desk. As he pulled out a checklist, he added, "But seriously, Bob, what's to keep that from happening here under your watch?"

"You are right, failure is always an option," Bob reflected. "But I will apply all that you've taught me. And with your permission, I'm asking you to keep me accountable. Call me, text me, anything. I welcome it, but I intend to keep things growing forward."

"Good answer," Jack said with a slight smile. "I'm glad to hear you ask for my help, for you know very well that I'm one to give it."

Flipping the folder closed, Jack laid the checklist beside it. "Now, I want you to take some final notes. Are you ready?" Jack asked.

"Fire away," Bob replied.

"The truth," Jack acknowledged, "is that leaders tell me all the time that they have what it takes. They try to convince themselves that everything will be okay—but as you know, failure is *always* an option if you don't plan, prepare, and execute. And even then, failure can still happen."

Jack leaned forward and continued, "You must know that there is no true failure unless you quit. Failing is definitely and always an option, but it's a stupid one, and one that you really do not want to try."

Bob was taking notes as fast as he could. After a pause to let him catch up, Jack pointed to an old painting on the wall and asked, "See that painting of the two seeds?"

Nodding, Bob studied it. He had seen it before: it depicted a blackened forest scene, with two brown seeds just under surface, and bits of green grass poking through the ground. The caption read:

"Every adversity, every failure, every heartache carries with it a seed of equal or greater benefit." – *Napoleon Hill*

"What is failure, anyway?" Jack asked. "The dictionary defines it as the condition of not achieving the desired end. If that is true, you have control over failure. What was the desired goal or result? You set the bar and the expectation. The opinion someone else has of you and your situation doesn't have to be your reality. It takes courage to not fail."

"And how would you define courage?" Bob asked, not looking up from his own notes.

"Courage is not letting your reality determine your reaction," Jack continued. "Don't let the possibility of failure control your destiny. So as you can see, failure is just a mindset, not a destiny."

"I think I got most of what you said," Bob admitted, looking up. "But if failure is a mindset, how can I avoid it?"

"You have to avoid the mindset of failing altogether, in every area of your life," Jack stated. "This practical list should help."

He cleared his throat and read:

- Be a great time manager

- Get up early and get going

- Be willing to work more hours than the normal guy

- Read more, for as Harry S. Truman used to say, "Leaders are readers, but not all readers are leaders."

- Listen to the best and mimic them

- Spend your time with the best

- Be selective about with whom you surround yourself

- Don't be complacent

- Always be evolving, adaptable to change

- Invest in yourself

- Grow forward

"Here is my final thought for you today," Jack said as he slid the checklist into the closed folder. "I'm going to ask you a question, but if you dig into the mindset, it is one of winning and accomplishment, not one of failure."

"Okay," Bob replied. "I'll give it a go."

"Would you rather have a million dollars or a million friends?" Jack asked.

After a few seconds, Bob answered, "No doubt this is a trick question, and though I'd like a million dollars, I'll say 'a million friends' is the correct answer."

"Yes, that is the correct answer, and here is why," Jack explained. "If you had a million friends, you could ask them each to give you a dollar and you would have both: the million friends and a million dollars! What's more, imagine what you could do if you had a million friends!"

As Bob stood up, Jack also stood, and they shook hands. "Success is a choice, my young friend," Jack offered as a final tribute. "It's a choice you make every single moment of every single day."

Bob was quiet as he left Jack's office. Much to think about…and much to put into practice as VP of operations.

If I Can Do It, Anyone Can

Alejandro

10

Several weeks later, Alejandro pulled his car in front of Jack's apartment. Jack was waiting.

"Do you have thirty minutes today for coffee and a scone?" Jack asked. "Then to my office."

"Sure, that works for me," Alejandro replied. The dreaded meeting with Jack was finally happening. For weeks he had evaded it, saying he was busy, but he knew he couldn't put it off forever. He wanted to say, "Let's get it over with," but he resisted the urge. His face, however, communicated his feelings well enough.

Alejandro had been mulling over and over in his mind what Jack had meant by saying that his uncle's success in the chauffeur business didn't guarantee that he, Alejandro, would succeed as well.

There are no guarantees. That was the crux of the matter.

Jack just smiled and talked about Raul and his improved health until they reached the coffee shop.

The line inside the café was shorter than usual, and the cheerful Cheri was behind the counter. "Oh, hey Jack, the regular?" she asked.

"Yes, but two of everything," Jack replied.

"Be right up," Cheri responded as she grabbed two scones and popped them in the microwave. The two coffees were on the counter moments later.

Jack paid while Alejandro cleared away the morning paper from two seats in the corner. They were thick cushioned chairs, but Jack didn't have to worry about Alejandro getting drowsy. They wouldn't be here long enough for that.

Sipping the hot coffee quietly while Jack situated his briefcase on the little table beside them, Alejandro was really starting to feel nervous.

"Before you start thinking too much," Jack interrupted, "I want to do most of the talking today, and I promise I won't hurt you—but you may want to take notes."

Handing Alejandro a small black leather notebook with a silver pen attached to it, Jack said, "Keep it as a gift from me...to your future!"

"Thanks," Alejandro replied. He clicked the pen a few times and smiled.

"I had it inscribed," Jack added.

"Oh, sure enough," Alejandro noted. He twisted the pen around in a slow circle. "It says, 'If you can conceive it, you can achieve it.' That's cool. Thank you."

"I hoped you would like it, and I'm going to make you use it," Jack responded. "I want to run through a few things while you take notes. Hit me with questions at any time. But we have less than thirty minutes, and I want to make it worth your while."

"Ok, go for it," Alejandro exclaimed as he flipped open his new notebook. This was already turning out a bit better than he had expected.

Jack took a gulp of coffee and began.

"Regarding the 'If I can do it, anyone can' myth, it's important that you know how to beat it. That means seeing through the person saying it and also living your life in the true reality of that phrase."

As Alejandro wrote, Jack continued. "When people say, 'if I can do it, anyone can,' it means one of three different things, each of them a reason for failure."

Failure Reason #1

"First, it means they do not really feel like they should be there—like they don't deserve to be there. It's a bit like the new CEO who got the job because his father died. Maybe that's an uncommon example, but the people who say this are usually not the fighters. They are the people who were given a head start."

"It's the old silver spoon concept, where someone inherited their wealth?" Alejandro asked.

"Yes, perhaps," replied Jack, "but it's more than that. The people who put in the time and have the determination to get up every single time they get knocked down rarely employ or even think about this myth, because they know there aren't many who would do what they did."

As Alejandro made notes, Jack continued. "In fact, this is more a clueless statement than anything. It's almost as though you were trekking through the jungle and said to your team, 'Hey guys, I just lost my compass…follow me!' Not good advice, and that person certainly is not going to be leading anybody anywhere. It's aimless. There is no direction, but hey, you can reach the stars!"

"I'm open to direction, for sure," Alejandro expounded. "But it had better lead me to a good destination."

"Leaders need to give directions, not aimless directives," Jack concluded. "The intent may not be malicious, but it's certainly clueless."

Failure Reason #2

"The second reason this sets people up for failure is because it misses the mark. Someone says 'if I can do it, anyone can' because they want to make you feel better, yet don't know what to say. Feeling better does not really make you any better, now does it?" Jack pointed out.

"No, it doesn't," Alejandro said, shaking his head.

"Your uncle probably said this hopefully, to keep you in the family business or to encourage you, but do you think he really meant it?" Jack pried. "In your heart, do you think his words applied to you?"

Alejandro stopped writing and looked up. "I know what you mean now, and I take no offense. I'll tell you how I feel about those words right now." As if searching for the right words to say, he continued, "I felt empty and hungry, like food arrived in my stomach but there was nothing there. I don't think he meant to hurt me, but his words really didn't help me."

"No doubt he meant well," Jack added. "But I think your description is an accurate one."

"Looking back on it," Alejandro reflected, "I bet he wanted to give me an opportunity to make money, and it was something he knew well, so he was probably looking at it and thinking, 'how hard can it be?'"

"Again, good points," Jack said in return. "I would agree with you. Now, there are people who use this myth because they are humbled by their own accomplishments and hope that others could catch on. These few people are just so positive they refuse to believe, or are naïve to the fact, that other people are not actually willing to do what they have done to achieve the same results. I know your uncle meant well, but I also don't think his success was an accident."

"That's for sure!" Alejandro stated emphatically. "Uncle Raul worked very hard to achieve the success he did. I can't tell you how many times he worked late, started early, pulled all-nighters, did his own mechanic work, and more. He's earned his success."

"And that is the point," Jack pointed out. "Raul is indeed a humble man, but he knows better than to say that you might accidentally find success. His success was the result of many factors, none of them accidental—principally his people skills and his determination, wouldn't you agree?"

"Absolutely," Alejandro noted. He was getting worked up himself, but it felt good to express his true feelings. Jack seemed to be listening and prying at the same time.

"Giving a person the false perspective that they can do something is not right," Jack continued. "It may be an attempt to make the person feel better, but it won't last. After all, if people really could, they would."

Alejandro held up his pen as if to ask a question. When Jack paused, Alejandro jumped in, "What about the fact that people spend so much time on Facebook, or playing games like Candy Crush, or making excuses for why they didn't make that sales call? If people worked harder, they would achieve more, there is no question about that."

"The thinking is that if people did everything right, they would be more successful," Jack reasoned along the thought train. "That is partly true, but not entirely. And sadly, that logic is what keeps the myth alive. It can't 100% be proven false, because the person hasn't been 100% on task—so they whip themselves in some manner and promise to try harder next time."

"That has been my challenge," Alejandro admitted. "I try to do everything right, but I really don't think I have what it takes to be the chauffeur my uncle is, which means I cannot be as successful as he has been."

"And you feel stuck and confused, and sheer hard work is your solution," Jack added.

"Bam!" Alejandro exclaimed, whacking his pen on his notebook. "I can't break the cycle, and then I think it's me, like I'm the one with the problem, as if I should know better or work even harder. But the fact is—maybe I don't actually want to be a chauffeur."

"To beat this myth, the truth must be known," Jack stated calmly as he sat a bit more forward in his chair. "You are a smart young man and your future is bright. You can see through the falsity of this myth, and though your uncle is truly humble, it takes much more to be a chauffeur than him saying, 'If I can do it, you can, too.' Isn't that the truth?"

Alejandro nodded vigorously as he chewed on the cold scone he had jammed in his mouth a moment before.

Failure Reason #3

"The third reason this myth sets people up for failure is the strongest one of all," Jack said as he glanced at his watch. Time was still in his favor. "Master manipulators use this myth all the time to motivate their 'understudies' to take action and perform better. It's a false promise of success that only serves the one telling the lie—they are manipulating you to believe it so that you will bring them a profit. That is selfish ambition at its finest. Remember the story I told you about the lady at the top of the real estate company?"

"Yes, I remember her," Alejandro acknowledged. "I could almost feel the tension in my spine as you were telling me that story, because I've sat in similar meetings, even in real estate meetings, where we've been pressured to perform better."

"Does it ever work, long term?" Jack asked with a sarcastic tone.

"Of course not," Alejandro replied. "But in the moment, everyone is pumped up and high-fiving each other and making unrealistic promises, but I swear, 24 hours later, things are worse off than before. When the hot air vanishes, some of the life has also been sucked out of the people."

"It's good that you can see it for what it is," Jack reasoned aloud. "Most people get caught up in the words and the ideas, while others simply turn off. Only a few can see it for what it is."

"What's that quote by Mark Twain about opening your mouth and proving you don't know anything?" Alejandro asked.

"You and I *are* on the same page," Jack responded with a chuckle. "That quote goes like this: 'It is better to keep your mouth closed and let people think you are a fool than to open it and remove all doubt.'"

"Exactly!" Alejandro laughed. "People want help and advice from those who have answers, but leaders should guard their words carefully, and certainly should not say things they don't really mean."

"How right you are," Jack said in response. "And the truth is that if anyone could do it, they would have already done it. Never forget that, as it is the surest way to prove the falsity of this myth."

In sum

Alejandro raised his pen again and asked, "So, the real estate owner—what could she have said on that stage to truly help her people?"

"Another good question," Jack nodded. "She should have praised them; told them that the company wouldn't be what it is without their help, which would of course be the truth. Train, motivate, and encourage, but don't lie. Pumping your employees up only sets them up for failure. That is never the way to effectively lead, build a business, or create anything of lasting value."

"What's more," Jack continued, "using this myth gives the illusion of humility, but is actually more manipulation than motivation, and that provides temporary results at best."

"I think the best way to fix this myth is to chart your own course," Alejandro interjected. "More specifically, I need to chart *my* own course."

"You nailed it!" Jack said in return. He finished the last swig of his coffee and glanced at his watch. Their thirty minutes had passed a few minutes ago.

They gathered up their items, placed their empty cups on the counter, and threw their napkins in the trash bin.

"Hey, I meant to tell you that Uncle Raul will be back on the road in a few short weeks," Alejandro explained as he pushed through the café's side exit door.

Jack couldn't tell by Alejandro's voice if the eventual return of his uncle was a good thing or a bad thing, so he didn't reply.

Two weeks later, on a Sunday evening, Jack received a text from Raul. It read:

I will pick you up tomorrow morning. Alejandro just quit. I'm guessing that you had something to do with this.

"What? Oh, great, now I've made mother bear angry!" Jack said aloud, placing his phone back on the counter.

"What is it, honey?" his wife asked. They were reading in the kitchen as they sipped hot tea, an evening treat they enjoyed together.

"You know that Raul has been in the hospital and that his nephew, Alejandro, has been driving his car for him, right?" Jack explained. "Well, I've been working with Alejandro for weeks. He was trying to fill his uncle's shoes because Raul had told him once, 'If I can do it, anyone can.' Those misguided words have been bugging Alejandro for years. Now I think he took action, and Raul is no doubt going to be fighting angry tomorrow morning."

Name It So You Can Claim It

11

Tricia

"**T**hank you again for meeting me here," Tricia said as Jack pulled out a chair at her table. "This little bistro is always pretty busy, but they take reservations, and that really helps with planning ahead."

"I'll remember that," Jack replied, placing his leather folder on the table. "Are you ready for today?"

"I hope so," Tricia admitted. "Last week you pretty much blew me and my theory out of the water! I can't believe that I used to think I could name it and claim it, write a goal on a piece of paper, put it in my wallet, and seriously expect it to happen all by itself."

"But you've recovered," Jack said encouragingly, trying to deflect her focus away from embarrassment and toward improvement.

"Yes, and with a vengeance," Tricia exclaimed. "I am so ready to finally get my hands on a goal-setting process that truly works."

Whether creatures of habit or because they liked what they chose last time, they both ordered the same meal and drinks as before, and then settled in for the mental battle.

The goal-setting process

"I base the goal-setting process on four separate steps," Jack began. "I'll outline them here so you have them for your notes, and then break them down so you can get a full-fledged grasp on each important step."

Tricia was poised to write.

Jack handed her a thin leather bookmark. "I inscribed them on something that I figured you would constantly have in front of you," he explained. The bookmark read:

> Step #1: Name It
> Step #2: Plan It
> Step #3: Work It
> Step #4: Claim It

"Seems innocent enough," Tricia responded, looking up. "But I'm guessing there is much more to it than meets the eye."

"That's always the case," Jack chuckled. "Now, what I want to do is go through each step and give you examples, stories, and teaching points that you can then assimilate into your own life. Then you'll be qualified to do this or teach this or whatever else you plan to do with it."

"I'm ready," Tricia exclaimed as Jack grabbed a quick gulp of his iced tea.

Step #1: Name It

"The first step you already know: naming what it is you are chasing after," Jack explained. "Decide on your goal and make it plain. This is far more complex than simply saying, 'I might as well do this' or 'I think I'll try that.' The act of naming is vital because it crystalizes your thinking, which brings focus, and then drive and determination in turn."

"Almost like dominoes in that if you get them lined up properly, they will all fall properly," Tricia added.

"Yes, and every step between the first domino and the last simply needs to be put in place; then, when you tip over the first, it's inevitable that your goal will be reached," Jack clarified.

"Hmm…" was all Tricia could stammer as she wrote feverishly.

"The goal that you folded up in your purse will not unfold itself, line up all the necessary steps, and cause itself to happen, now will it?" Jack asked. "A whole lot of planning, determination, passion, drive, accountability, and hard work go into the setting up of all the steps, the 'dominoes' as you called them."

"I had never thought about it quite like that," Tricia admitted.

"Goal setting is a mindset, just like any other commitment to success," Jack reasoned aloud. "It's not just about wanting some-thing really bad. It's about doing whatever it takes to reach your goal. I've heard of people setting up incredible domino displays that take days of preparation. They are incredible to see, but they don't set up themselves, do they?"

"No, they sure don't," Tricia said in return. "And the goal I folded up and put in my purse, it's not going to happen by itself either, that's what you're saying."

"And you know it!" Jack exclaimed. "Now, another thing to remember is that if you don't know where you're going, you'll end up anywhere. If you don't set goals to determine your own future and your own success, you'll end up serving someone else's goal. That may not be a bad thing, as long as that is also part of your own personal goal."

"Can you give me an example?" Tricia asked, trying to stay with his line of thinking.

"Let's say a young, college-aged guy wants to express his freedom; 'do his own thing.' He will eventually need lodging, among other things, so he rents an apartment, paying good money to the owner of the property and thus helping that landlord accomplish their goals of real estate appreciation, ownership, and future revenue."

Tricia could see where this was going, but she kept taking notes as fast as she could.

"He'll also need food and clothes, so he shops at the stores nearby, thus accomplishing the goals of the store owners," Jack added. "He'll probably buy a car on credit, thus paying the car dealership back many times over for his purchase, again accomplishing someone else's financial goals. And to afford all these things, he will have to get a job that pays him for the skills he possesses. It will probably be manual labor, based on the hours he gives. The business owner is again accomplishing his goals through this young man's participation."

"Ouch!" Tricia exclaimed. "But it's not bad to work for someone else."

"Of course not, and every business owner needs employees," Jack replied. "But until this young man figures out his passion—something he will only accomplish by clarifying what he wants to do with his life—the steps to get there will be fuzzy, aimless, and impossible to take."

"True," Tricia acknowledged. "It's out of focus because he doesn't *have* a focus. He doesn't know where he wants to go."

"Now, suppose he clarifies where he wants to go and his future job requires a college degree," Jack said with a smile. "You'll soon find him on the college campus, much to the delight of his parents I might add, but it wasn't going to happen until *he* decided to. Until he named it, he was someone else's pawn."

Step #2: Plan It

"The second step is to plan out your future success," Jack stated. "Let's take this young man who decided college was in his future. He will need to find a college that can give him the degree he wants.

He also needs to look at the cost for tuition, find grant or scholarship money, borrow from the government, or beg it of his parents. Then there's a place to stay, roommates, food, work, and more."

"Sounds intimidating," Tricia noted.

"It sure is, and there are a lot of steps to get from 'naming' his goal to walking across the stage and 'claiming' his diploma," Jack admitted, sitting forward in his chair. "But if you simply took those steps, would that diploma not be pretty much a given? Of course, he could get hit by a car on the way to class and that would end his dreams, but taking the steps that he and his professors plan out will lead him directly to his goal."

"Can you break this down a bit more?" Tricia asked. "I can see, in his case, how it would work—but not everyone's plan is as straight-forward as going to college."

"The act of planning is nothing more than listing what you need to do and identifying any obstacles that are in your way," Jack instructed. "List the items on a piece of paper or on your computer. Then, if individual items need to be broken into smaller parts, do that as well. Accomplish the pieces one-by-one, and that task is done!"

"So one of the dominoes in my earlier example would be the 'find a college that offers my degree' bullet point for this hypothetical college kid," Tricia expounded. "And every bullet point, every domino, goes on my to-do list."

"And once you have planned out all the necessary steps, all your dominoes will be in place," Jack finished her thought. "Adding another step here or there, as you become aware of their importance, is no big deal. You just insert them into your overall plan."

"The fact that it may take years to reach a goal is then a testament to the number of steps it will take to get there," Tricia added.

"Perhaps," Jacked noted. "But the biggest element is the sheer fact that you stayed with it and accomplished the goal. And if putting notes or pictures on your mirror, in your purse, or on your forehead are helpful reminders to keep plodding forward, then so be it. If it takes you that long to set up all those dominoes, then know that it's going to be an amazing show!"

"Now that is poetic," Tricia gushed. "I can see it in my mind, just how you have described!"

"Well, it is vitally important that you see where you are going," Jack replied. "Not only in your own goals, but in the goal-setting process as a mindset. It takes time for it to 'click' in your head, but once it does, you'll never be the same."

Step #3: Work It

"The third step is the act of working the items on your list. Some find this to be the hardest part of goal setting, while others find it the easiest," Jack explained.

"How so?" Tricia asked. This seemed to be her favorite method of digging for just a little bit more information—Jack could appreciate that.

"It's hard for some, because this is where the rubber meets the road, where they have to follow through on their plans," Jack reasoned. "But, armed with the same tasks, it's also considered to be the easiest because they know exactly what to do. Just stick to the plan, and things progress."

"I get it," Tricia nodded. "I'm more of a get-it-done type of person, so the prospect of marking items off my list really excites me."

"Now, admittedly, any single item on their list may be a big task," Jack noted with a touch of empathy. "They might start it and get pretty deep into it before they realize they may need other people or other pieces to complete the task."

"But they wouldn't know that if they had never started," Tricia added.

"Yes, exactly! Remember the story I told you last week about my client who bought his prized muscle car?" Jack asked, knowing that Tricia was tracking with him. "His biggest step was saving the money. Another big step was finding the right car, which he did through the help of a friend. He didn't have all the answers when he started, but he took all the steps that he could."

"And it came together, piece by piece," Tricia noted, nodding her head in agreement.

"For the most part, he had just those two big steps—but it took him years to accomplish them," Jack pointed out.

"Wow, that makes much more sense!" Tricia exclaimed. "He started, and that was vital. But the biggest and most practical thing to me was his act of saving. That could have been accomplished instantly if he chose to borrow the money, but if he wanted to reach his goal without going in debt, then the act of saving was an effective way to get there."

"This is where determination and perseverance really pay off," Jack noted. "And having the right friends who will help—not hinder—your pursuits. It's also a period of balance, as you can't forget to eat or exercise or sleep while you chase your dreams. I am a big proponent in cutting out distractions, such as TV, sports, video games, bar hopping, frat parties, dating, and the like. Of course, it's always your call, but sometimes it takes a season of great focus to make it to the other side. The individual task, or domino, may be a big one. I don't recommend that you live in such a state of separation from society forever, but certainly for a season."

"Whoa, that's all news to me," Tricia responded. "I'm writing all this down. I'll have to think it through later, but I can already see how some of my friends have been pulling me away from my goals, and how that could really have a massive negative impact on my life."

"Our fictional boy going to college," Jack brought up, slightly deflecting the pointedness of the conversation, "probably has a handful of friends who want him to party, stay up late, go to movies, spend his money, drink, and maybe even do drugs. Staying true to his goal will force him to make tough, but beneficial, decisions about his friends."

"Well said," Tricia added. "I've always felt that true friends will push me toward my goals and dreams."

"Very true," Jack stated, "but it is your responsibility to know where you are going, is it not?"

Tricia nodded.

"In his younger years, a friend of mine had the desire to write two books before he turned thirty years of age," Jack continued. "So he got busy and wrote two compilation books, bringing together a lot of talent on the given subjects. The end result, after hours and hours of writing, contacting, submitting, etc., was two published books by his 28th birthday."

"Quite an accomplishment," replied Tricia with a hint of longing in her voice.

"On a side note, the last time he checked, one of my friend's books was selling on Amazon for $0.01, so clearly it wasn't about the money," Jack smiled. "It was about the goal—and he accomplished it by taking the necessary steps that he outlined in his plan."

"The hard work part," Tricia floated.

"Yes, that is certainly often the case," Jack confirmed. "But in pieces, everything is possible. You can eat an elephant, one bite at a time. It's all doable."

Their meals were finished and their drinks had been refilled. The lunch hour was almost done, as was Jack.

Step #4: Claim It

"The last step is the act of claiming your goal, and this one will not magically appear before your eyes!" Jack said with a flourish. "It happens after all the dominoes fall, once you have done everything on your to-do list. No mystery there."

"It happens when you grab your goal by the horns and wrestle it to the ground," Tricia joked. "There is no mystery there, either."

"Well said," Jack chimed back. "The act of writing your goal down may be the missing step that you need to bring clarity to your list of goals. But still, there is planning and doing involved. Again, there is no mystery here. If it falls out of the sky and hits you on the head, *that's* a mystery."

"I see how the simple 'name it and claim it' approach is so mysterious and yet so impossible at the same time."

"It would be nice if things fell from the sky, wouldn't it?" Jack laughed. "We wanted lunch. We knew where we wanted to eat. We planned how to get here. And we were prepared to pay for it once it arrived. Then we took action and accomplished our goal—walked, sat, ate, and paid. The food is quite good here, by the way."

"Yes, thanks, I agree," Tricia motioned at their empty plates.

Jack rolled on, "Granted, it is possible that someone could have, unbeknownst to us, purchased two meals exactly as we ordered them, walked over to my office building, and handed them to us as we stepped outside. Technically that's possible, but probable? No way!"

"When you say it that way, I want to laugh at the absurdity of it," Tricia replied. "I think people really hope that mysterious fall-from-the-sky thing will happen to them."

"Of course they do, because it's easy, " Jack stated. "But something quickly gained in the beginning…"

"…is usually lost in the end," Tricia concluded.

To sum it up

"Would you say that taking ownership of your goals is the first step toward achieving them?" Tricia queried.

"I would agree with that, but let me add to it," Jack replied. "Nobody is going to go to college for you, go on a diet for you, or save up for that sports car for you. At a certain point, you have to say, 'It's my goal, and I'm going to go after it.' Nobody else will, and until then, you haven't even started yourself."

"That is good," Tricia answered, making notes as quickly as she could. Looking up, she laughed, "I think the idea of someone going on a diet for me is the most perfect example. Nobody would subject themselves to that effort, and even if they did, it wouldn't work. It's an impossible thing to do."

"In very much the same way as writing down a goal and putting it in your pocket. Most likely, it just ain't gonna happen," Jack encouraged, wanting to make sure he put the final nail in the coffin of this myth.

"Oh, for sure," Tricia responded. "This is exactly what I needed. Thank you."

"My pleasure," Jack replied, pushing in his chair as he gathered up his leather folder. "What are your next steps?"

Unsure if Jack was teasing her or not, Tricia explained, "I'm writing an article on goal setting for one of the papers here in the city, and I'm giving a speech in a few weeks at a large gathering of women. That's why I needed to talk to you and pick your brain. Your input is truly priceless."

"Again, glad to help," Jack repeated.

"There is something else," Tricia said, closing the door behind them and stepping up beside Jack on the busy sidewalk. "I was asked to speak to a civics club, one of those rich women's groups that need someone to motivate them once every six months—but I want to do more than just tell them stories. I want to give them something with meat on it, something that can really help."

"I commend you for your vision," Jack replied. "Hopefully what we discussed today will be the 'meat' that you wanted."

"I've also been asked to write a book for women, about overcoming things that weigh us down, and goal setting is such a common thing for us to trip over that it's going to be one of the chapters—or maybe the focus of the whole book!" Tricia explained.

"That's great," Jack said in return.

"I want you to co-author it with me," Tricia pleaded. "Would you consider that? I've already considered the obstacles and I would do most of the work—and it would help you reach more clients. And as for me, it fits well with my goals. I know what I want. I know the steps. And this book is part of the practical 'doing' of my goal. What do you think?"

"Hmm," was Jack's reply. It was his turn to be deep in thought. "Let me get back to you on that."

"Sounds totally fair," Tricia offered. "And next time we meet here, I hope to have a good story of my own to tell you."

"I look forward to it," Jack said with sincerity as they shook hands. "I really do."

Riding up the elevator, it was his turn to debate—dagger or chocolate for Eileen? "Co-authoring a book? You know how much time that will take?" he argued to himself.

As he reached his office, Eileen was talking on the phone again in her usual animated manner. He gave a nod as he walked by, still debating.

*I Tried
My Best*

Carol

12

The next time Carol called was at precisely 2 p.m. on Friday afternoon.

"Thank you for the gift package," Jack jumped in, before Carol could even extend a greeting. "I will enjoy the book, and my wife will enjoy the chocolate with me."

"Oh, you are welcome!" she exclaimed. "I sent that last week, after our first session."

"It's funny, but I can count all the thank-you-for-your-time gifts that I have received in my thirty years of business consulting—on one hand!" Jack acknowledged.

"Really?" Carol rebounded. "I see it as a very small way of thanking the people who have given good advice that I needed. A $20 gift for $2,000.00 worth of wisdom is, to me, a great deal!"

"Your logic is no doubt reflected in your success," Jack noted with satisfaction.

"I hope so! But I have to tell you, Jack, the past week has been amazing," Carol gushed. "I'm sure everyone says that to you, but after you and I put on our doctor scrubs and started diagnosing my patients, I really began to see things in a whole new light."

"It's certainly a good perspective, is it not?" Jack asked. "Funny you should say that. I mentioned what you and I were doing with a colleague at lunch the other day, and he told me a short story about himself that proves our point."

"I want to hear it," Carol stated.

"My friend, many years ago, was passed up for a promotion," Jack explained. "He did a good job, better than most people would have done, and people thought he was a shoe-in for the job—but looking back with honesty, he told me, 'I did not do my best. I could have devoted more of my time to preparing and working on the necessary relationships for that job. I really did not do my best.'"

"What was his takeaway?" Carol wondered. "I mean, what did he learn from it?"

"Good question, and that was what I asked as well," Jack noted. "My friend told me, 'From that point forward, I began to ask myself,

"What does my best really look like?'" I think that question is exactly what your patients need to be asking themselves."

"I like that," Carol replied as she typed on her keyboard. "And is that not about taking responsibility for your own actions?"

"Funny how we keep coming back to that truth," Jack chuckled. "Okay, now I have another story for you."

"You are full of stories today," Carol responded.

"This one is about a client from Oklahoma with whom I worked recently, and I think it serves as both a good learning lesson and a framework from which we can pull other truths that you can teach to your people," Jack explained.

Sitting back in his chair, Jack began, "Instead of wondering if you tried your best, my client's perspective is to ask, 'Have I exhausted all my possibilities?' It will make sense once you hear his story."

"That exact phrase, 'Have I exhausted all my possibilities?' is going on my office wall this afternoon!" Carol interjected.

Jack smiled to himself as he continued. "My client was trying to set one of those Guinness World Records by creating the world's largest lemonade. His feat included an almost 10-foot-tall cup made of fiberglass, which could hold over 840 gallons of freshly squeezed lemonade."

"That's huge," Carol noted.

"As the day of the event grew closer, the forecast included the possibility of rain, so a big tent was needed—but tents larger than

10×10 required a permit," Jack explained. "My client asked one of his assistants to get the permit, and an hour later he was told, 'It will take eight weeks to process.' When told there had to be a way, the assistant said those dreadful words: 'Well, I did my best.'"

"How typical is that?" Carol exclaimed. "Not only is the help worthless, but the county offices hide behind their mountainous processes and paperwork."

"Be that as it may, my client was not going to take it lying down," Jack persisted. "He said, 'I hit a big NO, so now what?' He called the city and they fed him the same line. He started asking his friends for help, and someone knew someone who worked for the city. He called her and she explained how it could be done in two weeks if the right people signed off on it."

"I hit those walls all the time," Carol said in an exasperated voice. "Short of bribes, it's tough to get things done sometimes."

"Apparently, the hardest part would be getting the permit office to sign off on it, my client learned. So he called and spent almost an hour on hold. At 10:30 in the morning, knowing face-to-face was the only option, he went to Chick-fil-A and ordered a tray of chicken nuggets and assorted sauces. He put it in a hot box, similar to those used in pizza delivery, and headed downtown."

"That chicken is like crack to some people!" Carol joked.

"Upon arrival, he asked to see the person he had been referred to, but the receptionist was rude and demanded to know if he had an appointment," Jack described. "When he told her that he did not, she said, 'Well, there is nothing I can do.' He explained that he was in a pinch and all he needed was five minutes. Apparently, boss-man was at lunch and wouldn't be back for hours."

"I'm getting upset as I listen," Carol noted. "I hope this ends well, because I'm more perturbed than anything."

"Hang on," Jack joked. "It does have a happy ending. Well, he was about to take his seat for his several-hour wait when he turned back to the receptionist and asked, 'Do you know if there is a homeless shelter nearby?' She wondered why, and he told her that he had a Chick-fil-A nugget tray in the car and, since he was going to be sitting there for a long time, it would go to waste if he didn't give it to hungry people. She leaned back in her chair and crossed her arms, saying sarcastically, 'Well, honey, you can leave it with me; I am hungry.' He didn't ask if she was serious. Moments later, he was back with the nugget tray. Placing it on the counter in front of her, he quickly took a seat in the waiting room chairs, which had clearly been designed for teens in a junior high. Three minutes later, she said, 'Another supervisor can see you now,' and fifteen minutes later he was out of there…with a signed permit!"

"Wow!" Carol exclaimed. "What was it your client said—'Have I exhausted all my possibilities?' That is great advice."

"Precisely," Jack responded. "To me, to try your best means that you have exhausted all your resources, all your time, all your connections, all your friends' connections, and all your possibilities. When you truly try your best, you will hit your goals."

"In other words, the 'I tried my best' phrase really shouldn't be uttered until it's a past tense, proven fact," Carol noted.

"Sadly, most people lead with it, because they hope it will stop any follow-up questions," Jack added. "It's really more of an excuse than an explanation of action. If you are creating a handbook, that should be in there."

"Yes, I am, and what you said is so simple yet logical," Carol replied.

"Speaking of mindset," Jack pointed out, "winning needs to be no matter what. Winning happens in the effort put forth, so trying your best should always be a forgone conclusion. That doesn't always mean the goal will be reached, but when pursued with a mindset that never even considers coming up short, success will be more likely."

"But when people have the weak-kneed 'I tried my best' excuse waiting in the wings, it's no wonder they don't get far," Carol added.

"Here are a few bullet points to add to your handbook," Jack said. "I think you'll enjoy them."

- Stop *trying* and start *doing*
- If opportunity never knocks, build a door and knock on it yourself
- If there is a wall in front of you, climb it, go around it, or ram it down
- Remove the phrase "try my best" from your vocabulary
- Recruit and hire people who are ready to "execute"
- Take it seriously, take responsibility, and get it done

- Ideas can come from the most unlikely places (a broken clock is right twice a day)

"It's not funny, but it's as if our work currency has changed from the old days," Jack continued.

"How so?" Carol asked.

"Well, what was 'minimum' in the old days is considered to be 'good' these days," Jack explained. "Teach your clients, 'If you do just a bit more, people will think you are amazing!' Every time they do this, the results will surpass expectations. And I promise you, you will see wild-eyed looks of surprise and happiness on their faces."

"I so look forward to that," Carol replied. "More than you know!"

"It will be as if they have been cured of what ails them," Jack noted with a sense of finality. "And truly, it will be thanks to you, Doctor Carol. See you next week."

PART FOUR

—)●(((O))(●(—

MYTHS
REPLACED

13 Bob

It was 4:55 p.m. on a Friday afternoon, and Jack was making a few notes to clarify his clients' needs for Monday's meetings when Eileen paged through.

"Jack, there is an invitation that just arrived for you. I think it's urgent, so be sure you get it before you leave today," she said.

"Thanks," Jack mumbled, his mechanical pencil still between his lips.

Then he stopped. An invitation? Urgent? "Hopefully it's not a party," Jack said to himself. "I really hate parties."

He finished up the last of his preparation ritual and then closed and locked his office. The locking part was really unnecessary, but that too had been ritualized.

Walking by the front desk, he saw the ornate invitation, accentuated with a blue bow, lying on the counter.

"Going to a ball?" Eileen asked with a mischievous smile.

"Hardly," Jack replied. "At least, I hope not. See you Monday."

He waved the invitation as a salute and boarded the elevator a moment later. Only then did he turn the letter over to read it:

> *You are invited tonight*
> *to a private dinner*
> *at Shakato's Grill*
> *in honor of Bob Flanery,*
> *VP of Operations,*
> *and his team!*

The elevator door opened with a whoosh and belched people out into the downstairs lobby. Nobody was waiting to go back up, so the doors quickly closed to retrieve more of those waiting on the countless floors above.

"So, Bob has done well," Jack said to himself as he folded the invitation and put it in his coat pocket. There was a slight drizzle blowing outside and the wait for a taxi would have been especially unpleasant if he didn't already have a car waiting for him in its usual spot.

The fact that he would be invited to a party tonight, with no prior warning, was not Bob's fault, but rather the father-in-law Dale's fault. That's how he worked…make a decision and jump! Nine times out of ten it ended up working in Dale's favor, and so it became his modus operandi.

Jack texted his wife that they had dinner plans. "It's been a few years since Dale invited us for a dinner," she texted back.

"We will enjoy it, I am sure," he replied.

Bob Flanery hits the mark

The advertising firm had booked the entirety of Shakato's Grill, which meant there would probably be in excess of one hundred people there.

"He must have done *really* well," Jack whispered to his wife as he held the taxi door open for her.

"I'm so proud of you," she returned. "Whatever this is all about, I know it wouldn't be happening if you hadn't done something. You saved his bacon back in the beginning. He still owes you."

"Perhaps," Jack smiled.

Bob was there as they came through the doors, and he ushered them to a large round table in the center of the room.

"So glad you both could come," he gushed. "So very glad!"

Moments later, there was the clinking of a spoon against a champagne glass.

"Attention, everyone," Dale bellowed above the din of the crowd. "Before you take your seats, I want to tell you how excited I am that we are here, because it means one thing: we hit it out of the park!"

There was applause, and Jack noticed that Bob was clapping heartily as well. It was indeed not all about him tonight, and that was a good sign.

"As a team, you turned three massive accounts into even larger successes," Dale told the crowd, as if they didn't already know. "I mean it when I say that I have never seen a team come together like you all have. It's exciting, because the success you have brought can easily be repeated!"

More thunderous applause and cheers.

"Finally, I want to tell you all how thankful, and proud, I am of our VP of Operations, Bob Flanery," Dale beamed. "A toast to him!"

The room was filled with the clinking of glasses and shouting and more clapping, then everyone began to find their seats as the white-coated restaurant staff began serving food and drinks.

Bob and his wife made it over to the center table where, after brief introductions, Bob slid a dark blue box across the table.

It was a pen case: Jack opened it. Inside was a matching gold-colored pen and pencil set. They both felt nicely balanced in Jack's fingers as he held them, one at a time.

Looking closely, Jack could see fine black italicized letters coiling around and around the pen and the pencil. He held the pen first at an angle and turned it slowly clockwise as he read:

Success is a choice and...

Then he picked up the pencil and turned it the same way. It read:

...I choose it every moment of every day.

"Well said," Jack replied, looking across the table at Bob and his wife.

"Thank you, for everything," Bob stated. He coughed once. For a moment, it seemed like he might cry, but it quickly passed. "I had no idea who you were or what you did for Dale in the past, but I must say that today is as much about you as it is about my team and me."

"It's always a pleasure," Jack responded, handing the small box to his wife. "It's what I do. But not everyone makes the change; not everyone does what you've done. You've pulled off quite a big win here, both for you and your team. You've done well."

Bob nodded, knowing that Jack wasn't quite done.

"Now, tomorrow..."

"Yes, I know," Bob laughed as he interrupted, "...is a whole new day, and I get to start over, making the right choices all over again. I know."

Jack smiled and lifted his champagne glass.

Dale had made the right move in bringing Bob in as VP of operations. Smart moves, every step of the way!

14 **Alejandro**

Morning came far too quickly for Jack. The text from Raul about Alejandro suddenly quitting the chauffeur business had been rattling around in his subconscious all night long.

It wasn't that Jack was a people-pleaser in the slightest! That had never been his problem.

"I can't really say I look forward to the confrontation," he told his wife as he put on his tie. "But once it starts, I'll not back down. I have just never been one of those brutish people who delight in fighting for fighting's sake. I would much rather find a workable solution than smear someone's face in the dirt."

"That's what makes you so good at what you do," his wife encouraged him. "Stiff upper lip! You have nothing to hide."

"Fact is, Alejandro is a leader," Jack reasoned out loud, buttoning up his coat. "He is interested in business and in real estate, and specifically in leading a team, not all the individual tasks. He likes people, but isn't an accountant-minded guy. He told me he wants to be part of a team of rehab and sales people within a real estate company."

"He will do great in the city," she replied.

"I think so, too," Jack said thoughtfully. "And if that's the case, then he really ought to quit chauffeuring!"

"It sounds like he has already done just that," she added as she handed him his briefcase.

"Yes, but that doesn't make mama bear any less angry, now does it?" Jack grumbled to himself. "I'll call you and let you know how it goes."

A quick kiss and he was out the door to find Raul waiting, right on time.

Raul is back

"Welcome back!" Jack shouted as he drew near. Swinging open the back door, he slapped Raul on the shoulder. "How are you feeling?"

"I feel great," Raul replied.

Edging into traffic, Raul jumped into a long-winded summary of his ulcer attack: the rush to the hospital, the surgery, what he was forced to eat, what they made him wear, and so on.

Jack listened, glad to have Raul back in his rightful position behind the wheel, but still waiting for the other shoe to drop.

Finally, after the routine café stop, Raul cleared his throat and looked in the rearview mirror.

"Alejandro quit this past weekend," he said.

"Yes, you texted me," Jack replied. He hadn't spoken with Alejandro yet, but knew it was just a matter of time before he called to discuss it.

"I hear that you and he talked a lot while I was gone," Raul prodded.

"Yes, we did," Jack responded. "He's a bright young man, don't you think?" Such questions, Jack knew, could really help to deflect focus.

"Alejandro told me all about it!" Raul jumped ahead. "And what's more, he said I should blame you."

"Oh, great!" Jack said, slapping the empty seat beside him.

"I have one thing to say," Raul said, looking in the mirror again. Then his stern face turned into a smile as he said, "And what I want to say is thank you!"

"Why is that?" Jack asked, not sure if mama bear was truly happy or if this was some ploy to lower his defenses.

"I have tried for years to encourage him to chase his own dreams," Raul explained. "He kept coming back to what was easy. To me, doing what I do is easy, and I told him so—but I knew that being a chauffeur wasn't for him."

Sensing that he truly might be out of the woods, Jack pressed, "But he says you told him, 'If I can do this, anyone can.' He took that as almost a directive, that he should do the same thing as you."

"He already corrected me on that one," Raul explained. "What I meant to say was, 'You can do anything in life, so don't settle for anything less than that.' Those would be my words to him today."

"Have you told him that?" Jack asked. "Those words would mean a lot to him."

"Actually, I did, this very morning," Raul responded. "He was going for an interview with a real estate company that works with the older-but-elegant areas of town."

"Really?" Jack said. "Sounds like a great fit for him."

"One more thing," Raul added, glancing over his shoulder. "Be expecting a call from him soon. He said you would be his first call on the way home from his interview today."

"That is one call I look forward to receiving," Jack replied, glancing down at his phone.

As they pulled up to the curb, Jack patted Raul's shoulder. "It's good to have you back, my friend."

"It's what I do," Raul responded.

"And me, too," Jack replied.

War averted, mama bear happy, and Alejandro in the job interview of a lifetime.

What a way to start a new week!

Name It So You Can Claim It

15 Tricia

After weeks of delay, Mrs. Fletcher scheduled her final appointment with Jack. Tricia, as she preferred to be called, had suddenly and unexpectedly become very busy.

"It's those articles she wrote in the newspaper; now everyone wants her to speak or do some sort of group discussion thing," Eileen explained. "I was able to finally schedule a lunch meeting between you two at the same bistro, but it's for today at noon. It's like we are flying standby these days."

"Count me in, and thanks for setting it up," Jack replied. Then he pushed the button on his desk phone to hang up.

Tricia had asked him to co-author a book with her when they last spoke, but since then she had not mentioned it. Was she serious about the proposal? The work required to create it would be intensive, as well as the time it would take to adequately market it.

"I take it seriously," Jack whispered to himself, glancing quickly out the window. "Obviously, she doesn't."

At twelve minutes to noon, Jack stepped out of his office, locked his door, and headed to the elevator. Eileen was not at her desk, but a pink "back at 1 p.m. after lunch" note was stuck on her phone.

Jack kept up a good pace and reached the bistro right on time. He ducked inside and headed to their regular spot. Stepping around a waiter, he realized suddenly that the table was occupied.

Tricia was there, with two other women. He could only see the backs of their heads.

He was about to turn away when Tricia glanced up. "Oh Jack, you are right on time!" she stammered as she jumped up and literally pushed him into the empty seat.

Eileen sat across from him, smiling.

"This is Eileen, whom you know," Tricia said. "And this is my mother. She and I have been catching up all morning, but she wanted to meet you before her next appointment. I gave her one of your books."

"Well, it's unexpected to be lunching with you," Jack replied to Eileen. "And it's a pleasure to meet the real Mrs. Fletcher."

With formal greetings taken care of, Jack sat down again.

"I wanted to meet the business coach who really lit a fire under my daughter's bottom," joked Mrs. Fletcher. "She has what it takes, I've known that for years, but over the last few months something really turned up the heat. She's not who she was."

"I'd wager she's the same person," Jack countered. "Just a bit more focused, like a laser. Those do get hot!"

"Yes, that's what it is, precisely," Mrs. Fletcher acknowledged. "I do have to run, but I also wanted to thank you for your invaluable contribution to our family."

"If you say so, then you are most welcome," Jack replied, a bit unsure as to why this was being stated with such grandiosity. Obviously, there were things he did not know.

After Mrs. Fletcher walked away, Jack sat down for the third time.

"Was this your plan?" Jack asked Eileen.

"Oh, no, it was Tricia's idea," Eileen replied. "But I must admit that I'm anxious to hear Tricia's update."

"Likewise, now that you mention it," Jack said, glancing over at Tricia, who was all smiles. "Tell us what has happened since you and I last had lunch…and tell us why you're so hard to reach these days!"

After they ordered, Tricia dove in. "It's quite a story, but I'll start at the top. Remember those articles I was working on for the local newspaper?"

"Yes, and I read both of them," Jack noted.

"Well, those articles lit the fire that led to at least two dozen speaking appointments this last month," Tricia explained. "It's been crazy. And one paper wants me to write an article once a month, on different topics, so that means I'm going to get even busier."

"That's great news," Jack replied. "And all this is in line with your goals, is it not?"

"Yes, very much so," Tricia confirmed. "And remember my speech to that boring civics group? Well, that turned out to be a bigger deal than I thought."

"How so?" Eileen asked eagerly. "I would have thought it was a dead end."

"I thought so, too," Tricia confided. "Well for starters, they want me to come back—but what's more, many of those ladies are married to captains of industry."

"And those doors are opening for you?" Jack asked.

"Oh, it's insane, in a good way!" Tricia exclaimed. "My cell phone was literally ringing before I left the room that day, and I'm still getting calls day and night. The reason, they say, is that I was able to convey a foundational truth in a very understandable manner, and I've become the 'spokesperson,' for lack of a better word, for much of the female workforce."

"What does that mean?" Eileen asked.

"It means big businesses are hiring me to train their people," Tricia replied. "And what is very neat for me is that their bottom line profits are already beginning to see an uptick."

"Very good," Jack responded. "I share the same excitement."

"I knew you would appreciate that," Tricia smiled in return. "I didn't know how important that was to me until it started happening. I get juiced knowing that the companies that actually put my training into practice are going to see real benefits."

"What else is happening?" Eileen asked as she took a bite of her sandwich.

"It turns out that several of the companies I've worked with want to hire me permanently," Tricia stated. "I don't think I'll take any offers just yet, but you should see the price tags that come with them!"

"Suddenly doors are open," Jack encouraged, glad to see that Tricia had received such good feedback already. "And you were writing a book, if I remember correctly." Jack wanted to ease into that discussion quietly, without seeming too concerned or upset.

"Yes, my book," Tricia acknowledged. "Sorry for being so quiet on that, but I decided I'm going to base several sections in the book, such as a chapter on goal setting, on our discussions. What's more, I'll do your chapters myself, and give you full credit. That way you won't have to do anything except maybe read it over once."

"That does sound intriguing," Jack admitted. "And given the time involved in such an endeavor, I could live with that."

"I figured you would appreciate that option," Tricia noted with satisfaction.

"Sounds cool," Eileen added.

"Oh, don't think you are escaping so easily, my friend," Tricia exclaimed. "I'm going to have a chapter on networking and building relationships, and I will be picking your brains for that, because it's something you do so well."

"Now I can read *your* book," Jack joked with Eileen.

"We can talk more about it later," Tricia directed. "Right now, I need to clarify an important detail with Jack."

"Okay, what is it?" Jack responded.

"Well, you know how you said it was okay to have a goal and then, for whatever reason, choose to delay that goal for a time?" Tricia began.

"Yes, and I stand by that," Jack stated. "Sometimes a goal needs to be put on pause: whether because you choose to do something else for a season, because it has taken another direction, or because you realize it's no longer a goal you want to pursue. It's okay, because you rule your goals, your goals don't rule you."

"Is there something you aren't telling us?" Eileen asked with a twinkle in her eye.

"That's why I wanted you both here today," Tricia said, clearing her throat before she continued. "One of the companies that has come knocking on my door is owned by Jonathon Becket, who just so happens to be a suitable bachelor that my mother has been trying to hook me up with for years. Well, we went out on a date last week—and another one yesterday."

"And?" Jack and Eileen asked in unison.

"I think I need to put my book on pause for a few months," Tricia replied. "Not because I don't want to write it, but because I'm going to be too busy."

"I see—so that's why your mother was thanking me like I had done something earth-shattering for your family," Jack laughed. "I get it now. She was talking marriage!"

"Perhaps," Tricia admitted sheepishly. "But I'm going to take it very, very slow."

"No doubt in line with your goals," Jack added.

"For sure!" Tricia returned. "And Eileen, I'm going to need you to help me with all the planning."

Jack knew his part in the lunch conversation was now over, lost as it submerged in the glorious ocean of marriage planning and every minute imaginable detail.

Later, after a few parting accolades and promises to keep in touch, Jack excused himself. Before he left the restaurant, he grabbed a waiter and ordered a single slice of double chocolate cake for Tricia and Eileen.

"Put a note on it that says, 'Eileen—dagger or chocolate? Definitely chocolate!' She will know what it means."

Then he headed out the door.

It was not only good to see people making the right choices, it was powerfully confirming to see the return on investment in their own lives.

"Makes the risks totally worth it," Jack muttered to himself as he stepped off the curb. "I can't complain."

Through tears of laughter and happiness, it took Eileen several minutes to explain the standing joke she had with Jack. Thankfully, Tricia had been an ideal client.

Carol

16

Returning to the office from a quick lunch, Jack noticed the blinking red light on his desk phone. After shrugging off his coat, he pressed the button.

"Jack, this is Carol, and I know we don't have our call until 2 p.m. today, but I wanted to tell you the great news: it's working! Call me if you can. If not, I'll give you all the details this afternoon. Bye!"

His watch showed it to be 12:45 p.m. Jack had checked his e-mails on his cell phone while waiting for lunch at his favorite food truck vendor.

"I hate suspense," he said to himself, punching the phone number to Carol's office.

When he got through, Carol immediately blurted out, "It's working!"

"What's working?" Jack asked, trying to calm her down just a bit. "Bring me up to speed. Remember, we are doctors doing research, so describe the results so far."

"Let me slip into my white lab coat," Carol said with a chuckle. "Okay, I have it on. Now, you know I've been spreading the word that saying 'I tried my best' is taboo around here. I've been training them every day as they come in, giving them the truth, in easily digestible bullet point form. And I've put signs up around the offices with a big X through those words. And you know what's happening?"

"What have you found?" Dr. Jack said, playing along.

"My phone is ringing off the hook. Businesses are calling from out of the blue!" Carol exclaimed. "Sorry, I didn't mean to get so worked up, but it truly is exciting. I thought this would be my undoing, but on the contrary, it has pushed my business forward by leaps and bounds."

"Well, they say 'awareness is the first step toward change,' and it's certainly proving true for you," Jack stated. "I must admit, seeing that in action is always a very encouraging thing."

"That's not all," Carol jumped in. "You know me, I track every-thing—that's what I do. And I've seen a 32% increase in part-time workers landing full-time work. Everyone loves that!"

"That's a huge jump," Jack replied. Now he was sitting on the edge of his chair.

"My work crews are outperforming everyone else, and they are actually being sought out," Carol added. "I had one of my temp workers come back to me just yesterday and say, 'My boss asked me, "Do you know anyone else who works like you? If you do, we'll hire them right away."' The door of opportunity stands open for these people, and what's extra cool is that they are coming from *my* company."

"You've freed them to outperform the world," Jack replied. "Well done!"

Stuck in the mud

"But it's not all rosy," Carol noted. "A couple weeks ago, I had several young people, in their mid-20s, come in here looking for work. They had so much IT experience it was crazy that they even came to me in the first place."

"What happened to them?" Jack asked.

"They got to hear my speech several times and were hired out last week. On Monday, they were back. They heard my speech again before they went out for a new job Tuesday morning…and they are back already. Nothing sticks for them."

"Like noodles on a wall," Jack said absent-mindedly. "I've heard that expression, and though I don't like it, I think it fits."

"Sadly, it does," Carol explained. "These IT geniuses have the goods and the skills. They could be making six figures within a year, but they won't stick with anything long enough. They keep coming back with 'I tried my best,' and that's the end of their employment stint."

"That *is* sad," Jack added.

"It gets worse," Carol quipped.

"It does?" Jack asked. "What did they do?"

"It's what they *didn't* do," Carol explained. "One businessman called and threatened me because of them. He said, 'If you send those guys to another company here in town and I hear about it, I'm going to spread the word about you.' He was so mad at the pitiful work they did that he saw them as actual threats to society."

"What can you do?" Jack wondered aloud. "I mean, this is a business you run."

"Oh, it's easy," Carol countered, her voice returning to a normal business tone. "I simply refuse to hire them anymore. If they get work, it's on their own."

"Safer that way," Jack responded.

"For sure, and the truth of the matter is it *needs* to be on their own—they have to make the personal choice to change, to do whatever it takes to grow up," Carol noted. "We need more of what Thomas Edison had: sheer perseverance. His great inventions, he said, were 1% inspiration and 99% perspiration."

"That powerful quote is printed on the key chain in my pocket at this very moment," Jack commented. "I had it engraved on a small disc decades ago so that I would never forget it."

"It's such a true statement," Carol added. "If young people today, or everyone else for that matter, understood that, then this 'I tried my best' epidemic would instantly end, people would find jobs, and businesses would notice a huge uptick in their profitability. I'm telling you, I've seen it happen!"

"I believe you," Jack soothed, sitting back in his chair. "I learned years ago that some will, some won't—and so what! It may seem harsh, but that's a fact of life. True change comes from within, and that always hinges on a choice."

"That is the case," Carol said in response. "I can teach them the truth and try my best to help them, but they have to choose to change for the better. And when they do, it's a beautiful thing!"

Jack gave an "uh-huh" in reply.

"One more exciting thing!" Carol stated.

"More good news?" Jack laughed.

"Other temp agencies, from miles and miles around, are calling to ask me to tell them my secret. Think I should?" Carol asked.

"You probably should," Jack stated. "After all, that's what you do. You speak the truth in a loving way, and you are getting great results. Go for it."

"Thanks, I planned on telling them all my secrets and my many words of wisdom…maybe I should charge and host an event," Carol chuckled. "So get ready for referrals—I'm sending them all to you! Gotta go, bye!"

And with that, she was gone.

Jack knew that sending referrals was one of Carol's ways to thank him. And he knew this was no hollow promise—his phone would soon be ringing off the hook.

He would take them all.

CONCLUSION

Jack flipped open a folder on his desk and made a note in it, checked off a few boxes that he had hand written beside the notes, and closed the folder.

"It's good to see the world is still full of crazy people," he said to the window. The one-legged pigeon was there again, bobbing its head along with an unknown tune. "It more than keeps me in business."

Then he touched the track pad to bring his screen up from sleep mode. He opened a document on his computer and began to type another chapter for his book. This book, like his last few, would prove to offend the stew out of people everywhere—and also bring in a lot more clients.

The fact that he had made the *New York Times* best seller list helped as well.

This new book would delve into the results of those who chose to change, who chose to listen to his counsel, and the amazing ROI that came from doing what his clients really wanted to do in the first place. He helped them change, and the results were nothing less than glorious!

The skies were overcast, illuminating the gray city buildings in drab blacks and whites.

"It's a beautiful day!" he murmured as he pecked away at the keys.

CPSIA information can be obtained
at www.ICGtesting.com
Printed in the USA
FSOW02n1438270616
22065FS